THE ABOLITION OF WAR

A
Center for
the Study of Democratic
Institutions
Book

WALTER MILLIS & JAMES REAL

The Abolition of
WAR

THE MACMILLAN COMPANY, NEW YORK

COLLIER-MACMILLAN LIMITED, LONDON

First Printing

The Macmillan Company, New York
Collier-Macmillan Canada Limited, Toronto, Ontario
Divisions of The Crowell-Collier Publishing Company

Printed in the United States of America

Library of Congress catalog card number: 63–11805

The authors are grateful to the following copyright
holders for the use of their material: *Foreign Affairs*
and Sir Solly Zuckerman for his article,
"Judgement and Control in Modern Warfare," in
Foreign Affairs, January, 1962; George Braziller, Inc.
for permission to quote from *The Tower and the Abyss*
by Erich Kahler.

ISBN 0 - 685 - 14563 - 8

THE ABOLITION OF WAR is a product of the Study of War and Democratic Institutions being undertaken by the Center for the Study of Democratic Institutions. The work was made possible, in part, by assistance from the Carnegie Endowment for International Peace and The Rockefeller Foundation. The Center, with headquarters in Santa Barbara, California, was established by the Fund for the Republic, Inc. Its work is concerned with clarifying questions of freedom and justice, especially those raised by the emerging power of twentieth-century institutions.

PREFACE

THROUGHOUT ALL OF HISTORY MAN HAS FOUGHT. MOST OF the time he has fought his environment to stay alive. But cracked skulls and the warclubs that did the work have been unearthed in almost every part of the globe, dating to the very beginnings of what we know about human residence on earth. Anger, fear, and avarice have apparently always been factors sufficiently strong in man's nature to divert him from the main business at hand to do violence to his kind.

In the beginning, and for untold eons, he appears to have fought largely for primitive, life-sustaining advantages —women, food, water, shelter. Yet, sometimes he indulged in the expenditure of energy and exposure to danger necessary to dispatch other men for other reasons. But even in these instances we can be fairly sure that the association between physical combat and access to or protection of these essentials of self-preservation was close.

At some point he organized, and in so doing, gradually introduced a whole new order of reasons for violence. He began, in a crude way, to kill for a series of motivations that moved further and further away from those that propelled him in the beginning. For example, he fought to prove his manhood, and went on to elaborate this peculiar compulsion through the whole history of initiation—proving himself as a "man." While a good deal of the energy and bloodshed of organized combat was still given to the acquisition or the defense of *things,* he had begun to fight for *theory;* over any one or combinations of the myriad ethnic differences of the species—color, religion, language, customs. He finally formalized this control system as a military organization to maintain his dominance over those alien to himself and his fellows, and came to call it "power." In doing so he elevated combat to an "art" and finally to a quasi-science. This last development raised a class of professionals to the charge of the system and even further abstracted the waging of wars for the common man in the field or in the hole in the ground. Now, finally, he fought most often not from immediate fear or immediate personal advantage, but for such vagaries as glory, national honor, and the Fatherland. He was reinforced skillfully by the artifacts of military togetherness—uniforms, flags, badges, and the trumpet and the drum. Thus manipulated and left to chew the crust of patriotism (however bitter and unnourishing it might sometimes be), the vast majority of men transferred

the responsibilities for the application of power to the kings
and the generals. Finally war, its complicated causes, conduct, and effects became so impossible of understanding by
the people themselves that the fighting men, supported
almost solely by the ancient myths and mystiques of the war
act itself, could look one another in the eye and quite
honestly vow to die for what they had not the remotest
idea of.

Throughout all this history of the development of organized violence, one must take note of the institution's
amazing accommodations to mythologies appropriate to the
time. It is a principal contention of this book that the apparently insuperable difficulties encountered in the renuncia-
tion of the war system revolve to a great extent on the
ingenious updating of ancient myths, incantations, and
propitiatory objects that have their roots in prehistoric time.
It is impossible not to note the resemblances between the
amalgamations of persons who possessed (or were thought
to possess) special powers that have been the media of the
courses to war to this very day: the warrior-medicine man,
the samurai-priest, the Prussian General Staff (which, having
itself constructed a viable god of war, consolidated the
practical and mystical functions into one image), and,
finally, the warrior-scientist combination. Each of these
conjugations of hero-figures meets the one requirement
for the ascent to and the maintenance of power—the possession of a body of knowledge or skills not widely shared
by the population as a whole. For example, one might
compare the similarity between the credence given to a

modern physicist pontificating on strategy or politics and that accorded an Aztec priest predicting tribal disasters and prescribing the requirements of salvation. This is not to say that these special persons have constituted the whole of the power organizations in any age or civilization. Nevertheless, in each age, the other power groups—merchants, bankers, kings, and legislative bodies—have found it imperative to merge with them and to share power with them—however grudgingly. Not only were their skills and knowledge necessary for the retention of power, but, above all, so was their mystique. So it is today.

One would think that the inutility of the nuclear-war system now and in the years to come would be indisputable, yet it is not. Powerful voices out of the new priesthood argue that ". . . if proper doctrine is followed, the consequences [of nuclear war] need not be disastrous to our survival, as is often supposed." [1] This statement is modern oracular rhetoric. "Proper doctrine" is the mystical prescription of the modern custodian of our war myths, doctrine heavily laced with the jargon of the sciences and demisciences. "Disaster" is interpreted in a similar, highly personal way much as the ancients might privately calculate the number of human sacrifices they deemed necessary to temper the wrath of the gods. Even the objects of war, the primary weapons such as supersonic aircraft and fourteen-story-high intercontinental missiles, suggest comparison to the mythological paraphernalia of past centuries and cul-

[1] Jacket statement, *Nuclear Weapons and Foreign Policy*, by H. A. Kissinger (Harper, 1957).

tures and hint at the totemic character hidden in the maze
of gadgetry and explosive. The weapons themselves are
made *not* to be used, and therefore succeed themselves in
"generations"—each larger and more powerful than its predecessor, and reminiscent of the awesome construction feats
of the Zapotec society that periodically built completely new,
larger, and more elaborate temples over perfectly adequate
existing structures. Even the names given to the mighty
weapons—Thor, Atlas, Nike-Hercules—suggest an almost
conscious recognition of the mythical cast of war, and seem
to carry a hint of invocation to power far beyond that contained in the instruments themselves.

If the war system is to be dismantled, the ancient shibboleths that help hold it together must be understood for
what they are. For one, the incantations that exhort men
to mass violence must be examined in the light of their agile
shifts from century to century and from culture to culture.
"For God, King and Country!" may have sufficed to move
the illiterate rabble of the eighteenth century wars to combat,
and the somewhat more explicit goals of "Make the World
Safe for Democracy" enough for the rally to arms in the
first part of this century. But what can we make of the
curious negative conundrum, "Would you rather be Red
or dead?" Is this not a tortured extension of the over-
simplified rallying cries coined for purposes of cohesion
rather than sensibility all through the modern history of
war—only, now couched in terms that leave the victim of
the war-cry-framed-as-a-question hoist between two choices
widely thought to be "unbearable"?

The uniqueness of such questions lies in their complete encompassing of current myth. In this seven-word confrontation the "enemy" is equated with that most dread of human conditions—death. It is framed so that there is really no appeal from the on-off answer demanded. It does not matter that the question is factually and emotionally preposterous; that in this age of megadeaths and megabucks few of us are likely to be invited to such an individual choice. Nor does it matter that no man who possesses a jot of humility for his own spiritual and physical frailty can predict with any certitude his behavior under intense duress. What does matter is that this kind of epithet-question slams the unwary victim into a position of unbearable emotional stress with maximum economy of verbal output. Savonarola and the Grand Inquisitor would have been envious.

Such cogent challenges may be unique to the thermonuclear age. Certainly they are propagandistic triumphs over the pallid facades invented for American and Allied consumption in World War II. The Four Freedoms failed to come to much, and remembering Pearl Harbor was something of a security problem. It was only out of Churchill's rhetoric that suitable exhortations could be culled for the participants in what was essentially a nineteenth century war. In our time we have seen men rally to the mesmeric cadence of *Al-gé-rie Fran-çaise* to butcher Moslem women in hope of provoking the Moslem Algerians to violence against the French Army. They slaughtered for a myth—the wistful dream that the colonial empire could be kept alive by bullets and bombs in this century. The Algerian myth we can see because of its microcosmic character. How can we examine those that clothe the greater and far more dangerous world, poised in ceaseless tension, susceptible to a thousand triggers, each guised as a "problem" or an "issue"?

Not easily, certainly, nor perhaps very well. But it seems vital to recognize the enormous power of myths and their subtle, shifting characteristics. It is important, too, to see that national or regional myths are not ridiculous to their believers. While it takes a good deal of emotional stamina to listen through a Soviet engineer's contention that there is a Marxist-Leninist dialectic built into machinery (this is why we have difficulty adapting to automation, while they do not!), it is just as trying to the Russian to grasp a lecture on individualism from an inhabitant of one of the most highly organized nations on earth.

A good part of this book deals with power: what it is, how it has traditionally been acquired and defended, and what it is used for. It becomes clear that ideas about power are inextricably intermingled with myth. Despite the sterile, impersonal character of the great modern weapons systems, designed to obliterate a country or continent thousands of miles away, where the adversary burns, fragments, vaporizes, or suffocates far beyond the sight or sound of his executioner, there remains the temptation to a new kind of mythmaking that is as virulent and deceptive as it was in the days of the bloody war club.

The new myths have taken on a peculiar character, which is founded on a scientific or pseudoscientific base. Their greatest threat lies in their pressure (as in every age) on the least understood of mechanisms, the human mind. There is heightened contemporary danger, however, in the sometimes reckless, always inadequate *pretense* that from the embryonic arts of psychology and psychiatry the actions and reactions of the human beings charged with the incomprehensible complexity of international weaponry can be gauged with certainty—that the human mind is understood. On this fragile base a school of civilian strategists [2] has invented a new approach to the war myth. Deterrence, the successor of the cruder American policy of massive retaliation, rests on deceptive psychological esoterica. For example, "credulity" or "credibility" are core words, yet no competent practitioner in the fields of behavioral science or neurological medicine would contend that credibility can be established with any two people of widely disparate cultures and conditioning by the same set of evidence. Yet with almost no reference to the paucity of knowledge of either mass social behavior under stress or individual power holders confronted by fear, threat, or lust, containment of the nuclear arsenals rests on the thesis that "rational" behavior is understood and, indeed, predictable.

The threats of the scientific-psychological myths are substantial. For one thing, they are largely propagated by the currently most believable segment of modern society, the scientist. The scientist is possessor of a style of presentation

[2] Herman Kahn is by far the most prolific inventor of these theses and coiner of words and phrases to explain and defend them. See his "Thinking About the Unthinkable," *Horizon*, June, 1962.

that parades as the "scientific method," implying a deeper, more orderly, more thorough and, indeed, much more innately *wise* method of reaching a basically nonscientific conclusion than is available to others. (Mr. Kahn's repeated references to "hard thinking," "detailed analysis," "skilled professional review," and so on, in both of his books are interesting examples of claim laying by one of the practitioners of the new professional invention, the operations analyst.) As a consequence, these analyses and arguments, covered with the patina of scientific methodology, have a good deal more viability in both the society at large—through the popular media—and in the councils of government than do the less formalized offerings of nonscientists. This is not to say that the scientist, in private research and in public service, has not in countless cases offered reasonable and often brilliant counsel for the preservation and ordering of the world. Yet, largely out of his assurances and professional speculations there is likely to calcify a new set of myths that add up to the same old credibility placed on war as the logical arbiter of international dispute. The computer-endorsed myth may well be the substitute for the passionate slogans that have for centuries helped drive men to the barricades and into the trenches. As always, the danger is that myth and power will be hitched in disastrous conjunction. The weapons systems (the hardware) are fairly well understood. What is not understood is the power hunger that resides in what the psychiatrist Kenneth Colby calls the "wetware"—the human brain about which we know very little except that it is composed of about 75 percent water. The myths that are forming up in the technological age rest the incalculable weight of the new annihilatory systems on this least understood of mechanisms, and reinforce our temptation to believe we can control the system we have built.

To write in one book about all the aspects of the modern dilemma is now impossible. It has become apparent that the establishment of the almost automatic war machine calls for nothing less than a complete examination of political, social, and economic conditions and practices all over the earth. Much written thus far has concentrated on military systems and strategies, with emphasis on the ephemeral search for "invulnerability." A few men, for example, Grenville Clark and Louis Sohn, have elected to undertake the more formidable task of examining the potentials of a world of law to replace the murder system. Others have contributed to thought and planning about disarmament and arms control. Still others have tried to envisage in detail models of the Western economy with the immense expenditures for the war establishment removed. This book is limited. It describes the ages in which war was an unavoidable—even creative—instrument necessary for the ordering of the world. It begins and concludes with the premise that this method of dealing with the world's problems is hopelessly outmoded.

Reference is made to the contemporary predicament, a state of affairs that is pushing all the great powers in directions they do not want to go and which, for America, can lead only to the continuing erection and maintenance of the fortress state, the price for which is loss of the very freedoms we are defending and the democratic goals we seek—both for ourselves and for others.

Myth and power are examined, not as new or novel ideas, but because these intertwined components of the human condition seem not to have had sufficient notice in a world bemused by its own technical virtuosity.

The problems are huge and sometimes deeply distressing to think about and work on. One is tempted by the word dilemma. Yet, on closer examination, it is clear that the means to abolish war forever, as well as the reasons for doing so, are already at hand. Immense difficulties remain in the actual construction of a world order that does not rest on the emotional convenience of military threat and counter-threat. Nevertheless, it is our belief that these problems can and will be solved and that the ingenuity of man will produce a workable substitute for legalized mass murder.

CONTENTS

THE ABOLITION OF WAR

CHAPTER ONE

THE WAR SYSTEM

IT IS THE CONTENTION OF THIS BOOK THAT THE WORLD HAS reached a point, no doubt for the first time in history, at which it is possible to think and talk seriously about the abolition of organized war. The very idea is temerarious. Throughout the millennia men have dreamed of and worked for the abolition of war, uniformly without avail. The institution of war is woven deeply into the whole fabric of our culture; it has played a necessary part in the creation of the culture, and without this institution the culture could not have taken its present form. Many today find it almost impossible even to conceive of a system of international relations not ultimately founded upon war. All this is fully recognized; indeed, the present argument is based upon the belief that only with the most realistic understanding of the nature and magnitude of the war problem can its possible solution be usefully discussed. Yet it is still contended that solutions are becoming possible. The demilitarization of the world and the abolition of war is at least beginning to enter the realm of practical statecraft and constructive discussion.

Organized war is among the most ancient, the most basic, and the most characteristically human of human institutions. Except by metaphor or analogy it is not found in the animal world. Violent struggle and the taking of life are, of course, common to all of animate nature. Among the social insects and the higher, pack-hunting mammals one encounters the group organization of violence, but it is not directed toward other groups of the same species. The wolf pack unites to bring down prey, not to fight other wolf packs. War, as the term is here used, is peculiar to man, just as are the other basic human institutions of religion, law, politics, or organized economic activity, with all of which it is very closely linked in origin and development. The priest-king-commander is a familiar figure in ancient civilizations, and many reminders of him survive in even the most democratic of modern societies. Like law or religion, war appears to be a necessary outgrowth of man's development of language, with the consequent ability to communicate and remember, and of his capacity for social organization and acculturation. War is a social institution, a rather special form of the organization of violence, developed by man precisely because he is man.

There may be differences of opinion as to the prevalence of war among the isolated tribes living in the empty continents before the dawn of either history or civilization. But even if there may have been primitive tribes to whom war was unknown, it is clearly a concomitant of all civilizations, even the most rudimentary, of which we have knowledge; and it is found among most of the surviving primitive groups today, sometimes in a highly developed form. As a social institution war is, to paraphrase one of Quincy Wright's definitions,[1] a *legally* recognized and accepted mode for the *violent* (usually lethal) resolution of issues between *groups*. Each of the italicized terms is significant. War is a legal, and legally recognized, activity; this distinguishes it from murder, riot, or abortive rebellion, as well as suggests its close connection with the parallel institutions of law and religion. War is an organization of lethal violence, which distinguishes it from pseudowar (such as the medieval tournament or the modern collegiate football game) as well as from the many other forms of conflict to which the name "war" is metaphorically applied. War, finally, is waged by and in the name of the group, which distinguishes it from personal quarrels, feuds, banditry, and other forms of "private war." Private war is really a contradiction in terms. War is the supremely "socialistic" activity. The death and agony the soldier inflicts, no less than those he suffers, are justified only in the name and interest of the community of which he is both a part and an agent. Nowhere is the principle of "from each according to his ability, to each according to his needs" so starkly exemplified as upon a battlefield. Except as a communal activity—an exertion by a whole greater than the sum of its individual parts—war makes no sense or justice; and it was probably from the sense of the embattled group or nation that men derived the mystic notion of the "corporation" that dominates so much of modern politics and

[1] In *A Study of War* (University of Chicago Press, 1942).

3

economics. Often, no doubt, conquerors have led their armies to the slaughter for the crassest reasons of personal or dynastic ambition; but they have been able to do so only in the name of something greater than themselves, only with the aid of some mystic, yet very real and operative, concept of a group interest transcending emperor and foot soldier alike. "England," Nelson's Trafalgar signal read, "expects every man to do his duty," and the "England" meant something great and valuable to the wretched inhabitants of the gundecks, who might be expected to profit least, if at all, from the continued prospering of the British landowning aristocracy, for which they were called upon to fight.

War is a system, or cultural pattern, for organizing and institutionalizing violence in intergroup relations. As such, to search for its "causes" seems rather idle. Wars have been fought for many reasons—for territory, slaves, booty, tribute, for personal or dynastic ambition, in support of religious or moral principles, for group freedom and for group "power" or dominance or "glory"—and sometimes seemingly for no reason at all except the conservation of the military institution itself. If this seems strange, it must be remembered that war has served many creative social purposes as well as destructive ones. Providing, as it has always done, an *ultima ratio* in intertribal or international affairs, it has made final decision possible in many issues that had to be decided, for good or ill, if society was to develop, but for which no other means of decision had been evolved. Within groups and nations it has had a powerfully unifying effect. The necessity for external defense (or attack) has built up internal cohesion and much of the great body of laws and traditions that hold the modern society together. Organized war has provided the cradle for organized economic systems. The great administrative empires of antiquity, which developed highly organized economies, could scarcely have been put together without war; while war has made many contributions to the development of the arts and technology. If wars, like those of the American Indian tribes before the advent of the Europeans, appear to have been waged more for the sake of the fighting than for anything else, it is doubtless because of the vital role fighting played in support of their social and cultural organization. One does not have to fall victim to the nineteenth century aberrations about the "survival of the fittest" or the "military virtues" to understand that war, as an institution, has had its very great creative functions.

Traditionally, the wars and military institutions of any given culture have attracted the major interest of historians; more recently the political, social, and economic historians may have tended to rebel against this preoccupation, but war and military institutions seem again to be asserting a high-priority claim upon the attention of the social student. This justifies the notion of a "war system," as specific to an age or culture as are its economic and legal systems. It is not enough to say that tribes or nations have always warred with one another. Even when at peace they have still lived within a characteristic war system, just as they have lived within characteristic legal or economic systems. The war system of any age or culture is compounded of many elements—the weapons available; the forms of military organization and command; the relation of the military function to the economic and political functions of the societies involved; the legal, customary, or ethical principles surrounding the military instrumentalities and largely governing their use. It is the total war system, usually beginning with the weapons available and rising through the political and ethical systems based upon them, that determines the place of war in the society, that puts limitations upon its use in the affairs of the groups or states concerned, and that defines the role of war in the larger problem of intergroup relations. And even when the nations, or groups, have lived in peace, the war system has deeply affected their internal structure as well as their external relations.

At least from the beginning of civilization, a culture's war system has been the most dramatic, and apparently the most determinative, of its institutional arrangements. There have been many such systems, which have often differed very widely. There are striking differences between the war systems developed by the ancient empires of the Middle East and those developed, at roughly the same stage of cultural progress, by the Incas and Aztecs in the Americas. There is little similarity between either of these and the war system in Roman times, symbolized by the tramp of the highly organized legions under standards emblazoned in the name of "The Senate and the People of Rome." There is still less between the Roman system and the feudal war system embodied in the knights and ragtag peasant levies of the petty kings and barons of the Middle Ages. If we live, as we do, under a modern war system, it is not that of the Egyptians, the ancient Persians, the Romans, the medieval feudatories, the Incas, or the Japanese daimyos. It is a circumstance that makes analogies drawn from one age to another as dangerous in the military as in other fields.

The war system under which we live today, which developed in Western Europe and now involves virtually the entire globe, is a consequence of the modern nation-state. It both shaped and was shaped by the emerging concepts of national organization, national independence and sovereignty, secular and nationally centralized government—all concepts that began to take operative form only about 1500. The modern war system thus hardly antedates that period. It is deeply embedded in the notion of the sovereign national state, a circumstance that makes it so difficult to envisage its abolition except through the abolition of the sovereign state and its replacement by a global system of law and government. The assumptions implicit in the modern war system are several. Since it was (as it apparently still is) impossible to incorporate the human family into a single universal organization, men would in general be organized into separate national units—the nation-states—each under a centralized and "sovereign" authority entitled to speak and act for the whole unit. The notion of sovereignty appears to be essential to this type of large-scale organization. It is necessary to provide the central governing authority with the "monopoly of [legal] force" required to keep order and enforce law within the body politic. It is equally necessary to enable the body politic to deal, as a whole, with the other bodies politic that, under this type of organization, must exist in the external world.

It might be interesting to compare the sovereignty enjoyed by the sixteenth century national "corporation" with that claimed (vis-à-vis its competitors, workers, and customers) by the large modern business corporation. Indeed, the chartered company, out of which the modern corporation grew, was normally endowed at its formation with sovereign functions, including those of waging war and maintaining fleets and armies for the purpose. In the nation-state the sovereign, whether king or parliament, kept order at home and defended or advanced the group interest abroad against other sovereigns. And his only means of doing the latter was, ultimately, through war or threat of war.

War and the threat of war were the only available means of regulating international relations, of getting definitive decision in matters that had to be decided, defending the group interest or expanding the group power. For a system like this to operate, there had to be responsible (and in some sense, representative) sovereigns who could not only make war but who could also be warred against. The sovereign represented his people in offense, but also spoke for them all in surrender. Civil law cannot operate with justice unless there are not only those who sue but also those against whom suit can be brought. The military relations of the nation-states could not operate with success unless there were sovereigns to win and also to be defeated. Violent rebellions introduced difficulties into the operation of the sovereign-state system that led to the development of a large corpus of international law. War was legal; rebellion, on its face, was not. When could a violent rebellion be recognized as possessing the legitimate "rights" of "belligerency"? The answer commonly turned on whether the leaders of the rebellion had a genuine "constituency" behind them—that is to say, whether they were fighting a war in the sense of a communal action, or merely engaging in sporadic riot or banditry—and whether they were "responsible," empowered to act for the rebel community, able to make its peace if defeated as well as to discharge its international obligations among other sovereigns if successful. The national sovereign was an essential element in the nation-state war system.

Though the system, as it developed in Europe through the seventeenth and eighteenth centuries, was generally "dominated" by one or two greater powers, it was made up of a considerable number of not too disparate units. In each, the sovereign, generally a king, enjoyed almost absolute authority over the conduct of foreign relations and war. In these departments he was not directly accountable. His freedom of action might be tempered by the advice of influential councillors or the resistance of taxpayers to providing him with the costs of war, but he was both commander-in-chief and the sole channel of communication with other sovereigns. To support him in his dealings with them, he was provided with a standing military establishment. In times of peace, no doubt, most of the "king's ships" might be paid off and the standing army kept at very low levels, but the permanent establishment remained, including an available professional officer corps, traditional command and staff systems, war and naval offices (or their early equivalents), depots, arsenals, and supply and dockyard organizations. Such establishments could be expanded to meet the exigencies of war as rapidly as the slow pace of communications required.

For war, the ranks were filled by various different devices, from volunteering through the compulsions of crimping, the press-gang, and drastic (though never universal) conscription. But even where compulsion was most prominent it did not (as in the modern universal-service army) produce the notion of a truly national force, an army "springing from the loins of the people," from it and of it and a part of it. The army, in the first place, was not the nation's but the king's. It was the instrument the nation handed over to him in order that he might perform his kingly duties. It was so little "national" and so largely professional or mercenary in character that most sixteenth, seventeenth, and eighteenth century armies contained high percentages of foreign soldiers —independent adventurers and "soldiers of fortune," or conscripts hired out by their own sovereign for service under another. In general, the recruitment systems, whether volunteer or compulsory, tended to absorb the riffraff, the worthless, the criminal or the aggressively antisocial, the poor and the ignorant, leaving the more solid citizenry to benefit by their sufferings. Ropp quotes a French minister of the time as arguing that each foreigner in the army was worth three Frenchmen: "One more for the French, one less for the enemy, and a Frenchman left to pay taxes." [2]

Such a statistical approach says as much about the war system of that period as do the statistical approaches of contemporary writers, like Herman Kahn, about the war system

[2] Theodore Ropp, *War in the Modern World* (Durham, N.C.: Duke University Press, 1959), p. 37.

of today. The armies of the period were instruments of the national will, not embodiments of it. They were small, the technology of the time not permitting the total outpourings of national energy that later became possible. Their manner of recruitment sieved them out from the main stream of the national life; their customarily long terms of service, from ten years up to life, isolated them from the community for which they fought and died. They were specialists, working at a dangerous trade, but one not much more dangerous than other occupations of a time when all life was rather chancy. The generals and admirals who managed their efforts (rather like the managers of modern industry) got all the honors, the applause, the titles, and pensions. The soldiers who did not die in service got a bare minimum of charity from the society they had served. They were mere cogs in the social machinery.[3]

This war system seems callous and inhuman; yet through-

---

[3] Or, regarded in another way, they were the champions of the society they fought for, much as a modern professional baseball team is, for a few brief afternoons, the champion of the community it represents. "There was no joy in Mudville; mighty Casey had struck out." The Middle Ages experimented with the very reasonable notion that since war is essentially a contest of champions, it might be reduced to the battle of two men, with the victory of one or the other deciding the issue. The idea failed presumably because the practical and emotional investment by the rival groups in the issues involved was too great to permit such a decision to be acceptable. A town or a college makes a certain, but on the whole very slight, emotional investment in its athletic team; defeat may cause it "no joy," but not enough pain or loss to drive it to resume the battle by other means. Until the end of the eighteenth century the nation-groups made too great an investment in international issues to accept the verdict of single combat, but too little to carry matters beyond the decisions capable of being rendered by the combat of the professional armies, or champions, whom they maintained to do their fighting for them.

out some three centuries it operated, on the whole, with great success. There were many wars, but (after the conclusion of the Thirty Years' War in 1648) no catastrophes. The three hundred years (roughly 1500–1800) witnessed a tremendous outpouring of creative and intellectual energy. They saw the great voyages, the colonization of America and the conquest of India, the beginning of the modern technological revolution, the beginnings of modern politics, economics, and finance, great advances in science, philosophy, and art. During this time the wars were not only incessant; within their scope they were bloody and brutal enough. But generally they wrought no such devasting dislocations as are associated with the Thirty Years' War, the Napoleonic Wars, or the global wars of the present century. In many ways their scope was limited. Fought by comparative handfuls of professionals and long-service adventurers, ex-criminals and pressed men, on battlefields measuring hardly more than a mile or two in dimension, over still rather empty terrain whose resources the armies had, to some extent, to conserve for their own use, they had relatively little impact upon the civil societies in whose name they were waged. Their devastations were not great, and beyond the immediate areas of operations the civil populations often hardly noticed that they were in progress.[4]

---

[4] Bred, as we are, to the concepts of modern nationalism, we often lose sight of the extent to which this has been true throughout history. The great wars of antiquity and the earlier Christian Era washed over populations to whom they meant little; this explains the ease with which alien dynasties or conquerors appropriated and often acculturated huge territories, imposing languages, architectural forms, or religion upon peasant masses, to whom one conqueror was much the same as another.

In the Europe of the sixteenth, seventeenth, and eighteenth centuries the larger states and many of the smaller ones enjoyed an underlying sense of security that often made the strategic, dynastic, or territorial issues over which their sovereigns fought seem of small consequence in the major stream of national life. Samuel Pepys, intimately involved as he was in his capacity as a high official of the naval administration of Charles II, could listen to the cannonading of the Dutch and British fleets in the Thames estuary without undue excitement:

8 June 1667: Up and to the office, where all the news this morning is, that the Dutch are come with a fleete of eighty sail to Harwich, and that guns were heard plain by Sir W. Rider's people at Bednall-greene, all yesterday even. So to the office; we all sat all morning and then home to dinner, where our dinner a ham of French bacon, boiled with pigeons, an excellent dish.

This entry opens Pepys's account of the burning of the British fleet in the Medway in mid-June, 1667. The whole, as it is given in the entries for the rest of the month, provides an illuminating thumbnail of the sociology of war in the seventeenth century. The Dutch raid produced a tremendous "flap" in London; and as the crisis rose Pepys's entries became a good deal less insouciant. But though he lay awake a couple of nights foreseeing the "ruin of us all," one gathers the impression that it was his personal ruin as a member of the responsible administration that bothered him, rather than any potential ruin to the nation. The peril did not, at any rate, interfere with his preoccupation with his finances, his meals, or his amours.

The countermeasures he helped to take are of interest. To outfit defensive fire ships required money—the king's, not the nation's money—of which little was available. Captains and owners of the needed vessels made difficulties. Officers appropriated boats needed for the defense in order to carry their personal goods out of danger. The seamen at Chatham and Sheerness not unreasonably refused to fight unless their "tickets" (pay warrants) were met; and when the Dutch offered to pay the warrants, many of them went aboard the Dutch vessels, where they were seen, brazenly "speaking English" and waving the enemy gold at their compatriots.

It was apparent that for the integrating nation-state this sort of thing would never do; and during the succeeding century matters were to be considerably tightened up. While desertion was to remain a major problem in all European national military establishments down to the French Revolution, disciplines were tightened to a point at which it was physically impossibly for seamen to go on strike (or go over to the enemy) for nonpayment of their tickets. The administrative bureaucracy was steadily improved in both competence and honesty. The problems of war finance and taxation were better met. By the middle of the eighteenth century the rising nation-state had provided itself with a reasonably compact and effective military organization and administration. But it still belonged to the king rather than to the nation. It was still at best an almost mechanical agent or instrument of royal policy rather than an embodiment of a national will. War was one of those disagreeable things that happened but really meant comparatively little in the lives of the people. When in the 1760's Laurence Sterne set off on his "Sentimental Journey" he quite forgot that France and England were at war, and so failed to provide himself with a passport. The omission caused him no significant difficulties.

"In England," Tom Paine (in *Common Sense*) scornfully exclaimed as this period was ending, "a king hath little more to do than to make war and give away places, which in plain terms is to impoverish the nation and set it about the ears." That the king, in "making war," was fulfilling a function as protector of the national security or defender of the vital national interest did not occur to the polemicist. Paine saw European military relationships as a "system of war and expense"—a war system, in other words, in much the same sense that the term is used here—with its own systemic consequences. In *The Rights of Man* he further developed the concept:

Whatever is the cause of taxes to a nation becomes also the means of revenue to a government. Every war terminates with the addition of taxes, and consequently with an addition of revenue; and in any event of war, in the manner they are now commenced and concluded, the power and interest of governments are increased.

War, therefore . . . becomes a principal part of the system of old governments; and to establish any mode to abolish war, however advantageous it might be to nations, would be to take from such government the most lucrative of its branches. The frivolous matters upon which war is made show the disposition and avidity of governments to uphold the system of war, and betray [reveal] the motives upon which they act.

15

It is curiously prophetic. How many have since noticed that every war leaves behind it a new plateau of taxes, a new centralization of government power; how many, looking back upon the seemingly "frivolous" causes of great military catastrophes, have blamed them upon the militarism of wicked governors! Paine's underlying concepts hardly differ from those the statesmen of the Wilsonian era were, over a century later, to bring to the solution of the war problem. His approach is echoed today by those who inveigh against the colossal military-industrial "juggernaut" that has arisen in our democratic midst to threaten our freedoms, to increase "the power and interest of government" as against the people, and to raise such apparent obstacles against "any mode to abolish war." Few of these have grasped the fact, as Paine did, that it was an institutional system with which they were attempting to deal. Unfortunately, Paine himself was to learn too late that his remedy—which was to abolish the system by abolishing the kings and "old governments"— might be worse than the disease.

As a mode of organizing the external relations of peoples, the ordered and limited eighteenth century war system had virtues Paine overlooked. And it was the virtues, rather than the vices, that were largely to perish in the great Age of Revolution, of which Paine was a leading architect. The nation-state, which had produced the relatively workable international system of limited, kingly wars for usually limited ends, had at the same time been generating new conditions, new and gigantic forces amid which the "system of war" as Paine described it could not survive.

CHAPTER TWO

THE NEW POLITICS, THE NEW TECHNOLOGY

IT WAS AGAINST THE HEAD OF A PERSONAL SOVEREIGN, "THE present King of Great Britain," George III, that Jefferson flung the great indictment of the Declaration of Independence. This accorded with the eighteenth century conventions. But, as Carl Becker pointed out, the real target was not the king; it was the king's ministers and the parliamentary majorities that supported them. This accorded with the realities of the new age of national organization, national unity, and national (rather than personal) sovereignty that the Declaration was to announce. In its final ringing paragraph the personal sovereign is dismissed from his ancient function in war and foreign affairs:

That these United Colonies are, and of Right ought to be Free and Independent States; . . . and that, as Free and Independent

States, they have full Power to levy War, conclude Peace, contract Alliances, establish Commerce, and do all other Acts and Things which Independent States may of right do.

In matters of war and foreign policy the king was dead; long live the state. The nation-state was evolving, by its own inner logic, into the national state, generating new concepts of national and popular sovereignty that were to render the old inoperative. When the Age of Revolution reached its end some forty years later, the military, no less than the political, social, economic, and technological foundations of the eighteenth century, had been transformed; and the eighteenth century war system was already an anachronism beyond effective revival.

Anachronisms often, of course, continue to stand long after the roots have been sapped from under them. It is never easy to detect the shifts in the foundations of social institutions; and since wars are usually sporadic occurrences it is more difficult to do so in the case of military institutions than of others. With the subsidence of the Napoleonic upheavals, there was the usual return toward the old ways. It might be said that the army that Britain sent to the Crimea in the 1850's did not differ greatly in structure or function from those sent to America in the 1770's. In many ways the nineteenth century continued to assume that its system of war and international relations was not essentially different from that of the old order, and to conduct its affairs in accordance with that assumption. In fact, the differences were profound.

The developing concepts of national and popular sovereignty had relieved the king of his unique power and responsibility in military and foreign affairs, transferring it, if not to the "people," at least to the government. Notions of liberty and popular sovereignty inevitably generated the popular army, like the patriot armies of the American Revolution. It was in the midst of that conflict that General Washington drew the distinction between "the usual contests of Empire and Ambition," and "such a cause as this, where the Object is neither Glory nor extent of territory, but a defense of all that is dear and valuable in Life."[1] From the popular army, fighting in a "cause" of such a character, there inevitably grew the conscript mass army—the "armed horde" of the French Revolutionary Wars, which so shocked the professionals of the time and has grieved most thoughtful military men ever since. As Foch, lecturing to the French War College in 1900, was to put it:

Truly, a new era had begun, that of national wars, unchecked in speed and scope (*aux allures déchaînées*) because they were to consecrate to the struggle all the resources of the nation; because they were to take as their goal not a dynastic interest, not the conquest or possession of a province, but the defense and propagation primarily of philosophical ideas, secondarily of principles of independence, of unity, of non-material advantages of various kinds; because they were to put at stake the interests and personal resources of every common soldier and consequently his sentiments and passions—that is to say, elements of force which up to then had gone unexploited.[2]

[1] John C. Fitzpatrick, ed., *The Writings of George Washington* (Washington, D.C.: GPO, 1931–1936), III, 359.

[2] Ferdinand Foch, *Des Principes de la Guerre* (Paris: Berger-Levrault, 1918 ed.) pp. 28–29. Foch added a footnote, pointing out that in the past it had been "wars of religion, wars of ideas, which led to the most violent struggles."

Such armies were no longer the mere instruments of kings or governments; they were the nation itself "in arms." As war was made the business of the whole nation, the whole nation was inevitably involved in the grim business of war. For a number of reasons the new armies were much larger and more devastating than their predecessors. The conscript was easier and cheaper to obtain (and to replace) than the long-service professional. The new techniques of politics and finance left the new national governments unembarrassed by the expedients to which the kings had been compelled to resort in order to raise their war chests. Technology, bearing the first fruits of the Industrial Revolution, made it possible to produce weapons in far greater numbers and to transport and supply much larger masses of men. It was providing the improved road nets and communication systems that made it possible to maneuver and command these masses. The typical eighteenth century army was a small force moving as a unit from one strategic point to another. The typical Napoleonic army, organized in divisions, was really a group of armies, each largely self-contained, which though normally combined at one place for the major battles, were separately maneuvered over wide stretches of territory, spreading both their power and their destruction across the face of Europe. Popular sovereignty had created, not the peace Tom Paine envisaged, but the new monster of popular war.

But the consequences to which all this was bound to lead were not apparent in 1815. The European powers were to fight about as many wars in the century after 1815 as they had in the century before 1793, but there was—with one important exception—no really great war to reveal the extent to which the old war system had been undermined by the rise of the popularly oriented national state, of the new politics, the new finance, and the new technology. The conscription systems from which the "armed horde" had sprung went more or less into abeyance after 1815; the national governments returned, like the kings before them, to a "balance of power" strategy founded upon the old concepts of professional war and professional diplomacy. While continuing steadily to equip themselves with the new political and technical resources that were to render the old system unusable, they continued at the same time to play the old game. They dressed themselves in the habiliments of eighteenth century kingship when kingship of that kind was no longer possible. They dealt with each other as personal sovereigns; the ambassadors they exchanged followed the rituals and obeyed the punctilios of an earlier age; the "laws of war" and of "neutrality," as derived from Grotius and Vattel, were still of operative significance to statesmen as well as to international lawyers, even as the subject matter such laws were supposed to control was changing under their eyes. On the eve of the First World War it could still be seriously argued, for example, that the development of the international law of neutrality was "in fact bringing the state system . . . nearer to the realization of the dream . . . of a community of nations just as much governed by legal methods as any community of civilized men." [3]

[3] Sir Thomas Barclay in *Encyclopædia Britannica,* 11th Ed. (1911).

The one really great war of the period was the American Civil War; and it supplied a true prevision of the future of war in the modern age. It was a war of peoples, involving and absorbing almost the whole energies of the two sides. It was a war of large armies, raised (in the later stages) by conscription, weaponed by an increasingly powerful and sophisticated technology, transported and supplied by steam power and commanded by telegraph. It was a war precipitated and sustained by propaganda and mass emotion; and fought not basically for territory or even economic interest, but (in Foch's words) for "the defense and propagation . . . of philosophical ideas, . . . of principles of independence, of unity, of non-material advantages." It was "unlimited" in both ends and means; it was waged, not simply between the champion armies, but directly against the people themselves—against the civilian material and emotional resources by which the armies were sustained. The effective northern naval blockade; the strategy of the Mississippi campaigns, which were aimed not primarily at the destruction of the southern armies, but at depriving the South of the human and material resources of Louisiana and Texas by "cutting the Confederacy in two"; the famous march of Sherman's "bummers" through Georgia and Sheridan's devastation of the Valley of Virginia, intended not only to deprive the southern armies of supplies but, quite consciously, to bring war home to the obstinate home fronts—all this was what is now called "strategic warfare," differing only in the still limited nature of the available weapons from the indescribable savageries the bombing airplane was to rain down upon the civil populations of Europe and Asia in the Second World War. It was a war that lasted much longer than anyone at the beginning had imagined that it could; its battles were unexpectedly, unbelievably bloody, and when at last it was over no one could clearly say how it had happened, what precisely were the "causes" for which it was fought, or how its results could justify the agonies it had imposed. In all this it accurately foretold the future; by 1865 the thoughtful could say that war was reaching the end of its utility as a regulator of the affairs of men. Some means other than this would have to be discovered.

But for many reasons the lesson went unread. Those who quote Sherman's famous dictum that "war is all hell" seldom remember that he immediately added, "But if it has to come, I am here." The national states continued to regard themselves as "there" and ready. While modern war was beginning to disclose its true and dreadful visage in America, the methodical and technically minded Prussians were forging out of the new conditions the astonishingly successful war machine with which, in the 1860's and 1870's, they were to unite Germany, humble the French, and establish themselves as the dominant European power.

The Franco-Prussian War mobilized the large numbers made possible by the new technology (and the new politics, with its conscription systems); casualties in the comparatively few battles that occurred were shockingly heavy, and it left behind it much emotional as well as some physical wreckage. Nevertheless, it was a war "limited" both in intent and in effect. It was short; it achieved a neat and what at the time seemed a reasonably viable peace; it settled the immediate power issue between the French and German military systems out of which it had arisen. It produced, in other words, a *decision*—in matters that had to be decided—without tearing the vitals of Western society apart. It dramatically shifted the European power balances, but it did not seem to have worked much real difference in the European system. The foreign offices, the parliaments, the press, the cafés, the bankers and businessmen, went on much as before. Even the Paris Commune, a consequence of the war, seemed to leave little permanent effect behind it. This nineteenth century modification of the eighteenth century principles of war and policy seemed to represent not only a "natural" and inevitable mode in the relations of states but also an entirely feasible one. This was to prove an illusion.

Unfortunately, the soldiers and the politicians and the power myths on which they operated also went on as before. From the Franco-Prussian War one can trace a swiftly moving linear development to the great catastrophe of 1914, in which the nineteenth century "system of war and expence" was to perish as irretrievably as had the eighteenth century system in the wars of Napoleon. The technically competent Prussians had provided against every contigency except the one that in war is inevitable—imitation. The Prussian military success in 1870—1871 was really a "one-shot" exploit, a sufficient solution to the particular military-political problem to which it was applied, but, as others began to learn its "lessons," inadequate to sustain a permanent military or political posture. After 1870 the conscript mass army system perfected by the Prussians, with its ready reserve formations, capable of putting a whole nation promptly "in arms," was copied everywhere upon the Continent. The Prussian Great General Staff, which had so brilliantly welded the new technology to the old concepts of war, was imitated with more or less success by all the major military powers. The Germans had no monopoly on the new weapons technology—magazine rifles, machine guns, military rail transport, telegraphy and primitive radio communications and all the rest of it. Krupp (which in any event had been quite willing to sell its wares wherever a market might be found) was but one of the great private arms makers putting their individual enterprise at the service of governments. The brash new German Empire had achieved "dominance" on the Continent; but in doing so it had failed to win either the military or the political security for which it had aimed.

The Prussians had not entered the war with the deliberate purpose of annexing Alsace-Lorraine; it was the passion raised by the war itself and that ancient (and uniformly fatal) hope of rendering "this kind of thing forever impossible" that made the appropriation of the two provinces and their fortress systems politically unavoidable. And this exposed them to the destruction that was to overtake them a generation later. The First World War is often ascribed to the "victor's peace" of 1871, which left the French with an unappeasable desire to recover the provinces and achieve a *revanche* that would reestablish the "dominance" from which they had been ejected. But whence did these unappeasable desires arise? In the light of later settlements, that of 1871 still seems rather notably moderate; and one cannot help feeling that an earlier generation of Frenchmen, confronted by a settlement of this sort made on their behalf by their king, would have acquiesced with no great difficulty. But by the mid-nineteenth century the "security" at which Bismarck and Moltke aimed was no longer attainable by such methods; the new Empire, in achieving its "dominance," had unleashed not only political but popular and technical forces that added to the basic insecurity of its position and made the dominance at best somewhat shadowy. These forces arose out of the developing nineteenth century system of war and politics that the Germans had raised to such a seeming state of perfection but that was already digging its own grave. It was already growing dangerous to attempt a military resolution of issues that the development of the war system itself was rendering increasingly insoluble by military means.

As the nineteenth century drew to its close, this peculiar situation did not escape the attention of the thoughtful. One may, it is true, marvel at the levity with which even responsible statesmanship confronted the tragic problem of war. Youth and ignorance may account for the lighthearted way in which people like Kipling, the young Winston Churchill, or the young Theodore Roosevelt talked of war; but the more sober philosophers of the subject, like Mahan, or Henderson in Britain or the industrious German theorists, seem hardly less naïve today. Even the diplomatists, who could really see their countries being brought "to the brink of war" over the most minor of contretemps—the Venezuelan incident of 1895, Fashoda in 1898, the Agadir crisis, and dozens of others—appear to have been almost equally unaware of the enormous explosive powers accumulating in their hands. But they were beginning to learn.

As the implications of the new weaponry and the new mass armies were more closely studied, war more and more began to seem too dangerous, and too probably unfruitful, to be risked. On the conclusion of the nineteenth century wars of national unification, the massive new national units they had created tended to retire from the practice of war to the mere *threat* of war as the basic "instrument of policy." More and more the great military establishments took on a purely defensive cast. Bismarck devoted himself to stabilizing a military-political balance, not aggressively to overthrowing one. It was the "aggressive" Germans who could later truthfully, if a little plaintively, argue that they were the one great power that had fought no wars at all in the forty-year period between 1871 and 1914. Yet the underlying difficulty remained. Germany could not stabilize her own power position without its becoming a threat to all the rest. In acquiring the power with which she could defend herself, Germany also acquired a military position which was a constant menace to all the others, and the others were forced by the insane logic of the war system to build their answering alliances, armaments, and power positions. The last decades of the nineteenth and the first decade of the twentieth century went into an elaborate game of balance and counterbalance, threat and counterthreat, that no one could ever win but from which no one felt that he ever dared resign.

It seems significant that the game was largely played, not

on the explosive Continent of Europe, but in the relatively undangerous operations of colonial warfare. The Franco-Prussian War ended in 1871. Astutely encouraged by Bismarck himself, the last great era of European imperialist expansion (in which even the United States was to join) opened about 1880, when the British occupation of Egypt triggered the African "scramble." The forces and motives behind the colonial wars were of course mixed, as always. But it seems clear that they were not predominantly economic—the economic rewards proved, indeed, to be quite meager—so much as strategic. In the eighteenth century France and Britain had fought major wars (by the standards of the time) in both India and North America as well as on the Continent. In the last imperialist era there were no wars among the great powers—either at home or abroad. The impelling drives were not, generally speaking, for territory, markets, or raw materials; they were for prestige, power, and "security" against the putative great war *in Europe*.

One may go back as far as the French occupation of Algeria in the 1830's. This flowed less from any lust for the resources of Algeria than from a desire to reestablish French prestige and power on the European stage. The French could no longer invade the Germanies as Napoleon had done; their governmental and military elites had to fortify their power and prestige by invading someone, and Algeria offered a convenient target. Much the same thing was to happen a century later when Mussolini descended upon Ethiopia. The new Italian armaments, the martial exercises and motivations, the claims to military prestige and glory in Europe, had palled; to have any effect upon the larger stage, all this military machinery and military drama had to be released on someone, however weak.

But less histrionic policies really came down to much the same thing in the end. The British occupation of Egypt in 1880, unlike Mussolini's adventure in Ethiopia, was undertaken only with great reluctance by the government of the day. The diplomatic history was, as usual, complex, but the basic motive seems to have been the necessity of protecting the Suez Canal route to India—not, obviously, against the weak Turkish and Arab powers in the area but in the event of a war with Russia, Germany, France, or Italy, the other powerful members of the European war system. The British secured their canal route to India, but at the expense of French prestige. The French reacted by their exploitation of West Africa and by pushing on to the headwaters of the Nile. But control of the Upper Nile meant control of the delta and, again, of the canal; the result was the Fashoda incident in which the two powers stood, or thought they stood, "on the brink of war" over desert wastes of negligible value in themselves but of seeming strategic importance in the event of the potential great war in Europe.

The Boer War was again basically strategic in origin. As Egypt secured the canal route to India, Britain's Cape Colony had long secured the older route by way of Good Hope. It was Britain's strategic interest, both at the Cape itself and in the larger game of European power and politics, that made the Boer question ultimately insoluble. The German emperor's famous "Kruger telegram" was a strategic move on the bigger stage; and Britain's interest in South Africa could not be sacrificed because that would too greatly have diminished her prestige on the greater European board. The later problems in China were of much the same kind. Visions of rich Chinese trade no doubt encouraged all the powers in their scramble for leaseholds; but it was the essentially strategic demand for a warm-water port and secure communications with eastern Siberia that urged on the Russians; and it was considerations more of power and prestige in the European context, rather than of material rewards in Asia, that led the others to attempt to forestall Russia by securing leases of their own or, in the end, by calling in the United States to declare an "open door" that, whatever its commercial consequences, promised at least to keep the power balances even.

It does not seem fantastic to suggest that the "colonial wars" after 1880, and even more the diplomacy that sought to regularize them and fit them into the new power patterns without precipitating a general catastrophe, represent, to paraphrase Clausewitz, a kind of "continuation of major war by other means." Major war was becoming more and more fearsomely dangerous and destructive; the great states were becoming more and more hesitant about fighting each other. They were all tending to take refuge in defensive armaments, defensive alliances, defensive diplomatic combinations that would preserve their military power positions in the face of technological and political changes that were rendering the hope abortive. It was as if, while clinging to all the basic assumptions of the war system, they were trying to make it work to ends less disastrous than those it promised even then.

As the decade advanced, the task became obviously more difficult. John Hay could still speak of our conflict with Spain in 1898 as that "splendid little war." The South African War that followed in 1899 proved not to be so "little" and very far from "splendid." Five years later the Russo-Japanese War—a "peripheral" conflict between "the Colossus of the North" and "Little Japan," an Asian power that was assumed on that account to have no place in the big European league —proved to be a major conflict, which nearly wrecked the czarist empire and again altered all the power balances. With the Balkan Wars in 1912–1913, large-scale major conflict once more came back from the seemingly safe periphery to the continent of Europe, and left uneasiness in its wake.

If the colonial operations and the diplomatic maneuvers attending them represented a continuation of major war by other means, they still could not evade the fundamental tragedy. All such efforts to find militarily based solutions for the problems resulting from the development of the war system only aggravated the disease. The British had easily stood aloof from the Franco-Prussian War, confident in their seagirt isolation and not greatly concerned over the outcome. A generation later they were being compelled to face the fact that isolation was no longer possible, and were committing themselves, however reluctantly, to the Continental war complex. The Boer War revealed the technical incompetence of the antiquated British military machine; and the British were extensively to revamp and to reorganize it in the following years. It has been said that it was only the lessons of the Boer War that enabled Great Britain to withstand the storm that was to break a decade later. There is, however, another possible way of looking at it. The two "little wars" at the turn of the century served to precipitate both Britain and ultimately the United States into the European system of highly developed, expertly led, and technically superequipped mass popular warfare that was by that time well established on the Continent. And the Russo-Japanese War (1904–1905), a much greater conflict in which the new weaponry and new methods began to appear, rather clearly suggested the consequences to which that system was leading.

The new firepower put an end to the old-fashioned frontal assault with bayonet and brute courage; operations could proceed only by the tactics of digging in and flanking envelopment, foreshadowing the dreadful trench-warfare stalemate of 1915–1917. And it was decided in the end less by battle action than by the revolution it precipitated in Russia and by the Japanese approach to the limits of their strength. In South Africa a few years before the British had won their formal war in the first year, only to spend the next three trying to subdue the Boer guerrilla horsemen who did not know when they had been beaten. The United States had a similar experience; its formal capture of the Philippines in 1898 brought it only an exhausting and embarrassing guerrilla war. The organized war system was losing its powers of decision at the same time that it was piling up its costs and agonies. The combination of popular sovereignty with technology (of "Rousseau with James Watt," as Fuller has put it) had already gone far toward undermining the significance of organized war in the affairs of men; military bloodshed was already tending toward a horrible deadlock from which political, psychological, and emotional factors could alone retrieve it.

The fact that the European war system was destroying itself through the forty years from 1870 to 1914 can now be read in the history. It was less apparent at the time; but there were some, at least, who quite clearly grasped it. It was in 1897 that the Polish banker and businessman Ivan S. Bloch[4] published a seven-volume analytical and statistical study of the war system: *The Future of War, in Its Technical, Political and Economic Relations*. Bloch's avowed and at that time remarkable purpose was to prove that war had no future. His thesis, developed nearly three-quarters of a century ago, does not differ basically from that of the present book, though he had much less convincing evidence on which to demonstrate it. It was that major war had already, "through the natural and normal development of the art or science of warfare," become impossible except at the price of suicide. "The very development that has taken place in the mechanism of war has rendered war an impracticable operation. The dimensions of modern armaments and the organization of society have rendered its prosecution an economic impossibility"; it was technically unfeasible from the military point of view, while if the attempt were made to resort to it the

---

[4] The name is spelled variously. To the confusion of students, the New York Public Library uses the Slavic form "Bliokh" in its listings.

"inevitable" result would be a "catastrophe which would destroy all existing political organization." [5]

The detailed strategic, economic, and political predictions that Bloch confidently drew from his statistical analyses were seldom to be borne out. The Great War "that has haunted the imagination of mankind for the last thirty years," proved less "impossible," and the catastrophe that duly resulted from it less complete, than Bloch had anticipated. Yet catastrophe did occur; and in Bloch's own state, Russia, it was complete enough to justify his prophecy. Bloch's was one of those interesting minds that can be fantastically wrong in the moment that they are magnificently right. His dictum that "the outward and visible sign of the end of war was the introduction of the magazine rifle" was sententious overstatement; yet the magazine rifle was in fact an important step in the linear technological process that was to produce the multimegaton bomb. If he did not see clearly in detail, he at least saw the broad consequences of the new weaponry with much greater prescience than did the soldiers who were inventing and manipulating it. Bloch, the amateur of war, is chiefly remembered today for the general accuracy with which he foretold the character of the First World War. One can find most of it in his writings. The unendurable new firepower: "At first there will be increased slaughter—increased slaugh-

---

[5] I. S. Bloch, *The Future of War* (Boston, Ginn & Co., 1902), p. xi. Bloch's work aroused the enthusiasm of W. T. Stead, the English journalist, who interviewed Bloch at length and in 1899 secured the publication of an English translation of the sixth volume, together with a long introductory report of his interviews and a preface by Bloch. The Boston edition, from which the present quotations are taken, is a reissue, with some new material, of the 1899 volume.

ter on so terrible a scale that it will be impossible to get troops to push the battle to a decisive issue." [6] The flight into trench and siege warfare: "Certainly, everybody will be entrenched in the next war. . . . The first thing every man will have to do will be to dig a hole in the ground. Battles will last for days, and at the end it is very doubtful whether any decisive victory can be gained." [7] The disappearance of cavalry (of which the soldiers were not to be convinced until the war was half over). The political strains: On the "sensitive" populations of modern Europe "you are going to inflict the miseries of hunger and all the horrors of war. . . . At the same time, you will expose your governing and directing classes to more than decimation at the hands of the enemy's sharpshooters. How long do you think your social fabric will remain stable under such circumstances?" [8]

Bloch's conclusion was that at which so many have arrived today: "War, therefore, has become impossible except at the price of suicide"; and "when the impossibility of resorting to war for the decision of international quarrels is apparent to all, other means will be devised." [9]

All this was, in 1897, astonishing doctrine. It is doubtless too much to say, as did one commentator, that "it startled all serious thinkers in Europe," but it had a direct impact upon at least one who wielded great power. Largely influenced, it is believed, by Bloch's argument, the Czar of Russia, Nicholas II, in 1898 issued his call to the world's first general disarmament conference.

[6] *Op. cit.,* p. xvi.
[7] *Op. cit.,* p. xxvii.
[8] *Op. cit.,* pp. xlix–l.
[9] *Op. cit.,* pp. xxxi and lxxix.

The Imperial Rescript of August 24, 1898, described the situation at which the world had by that time arrived in words one would hardly alter if applying them to the contemporary scene today:

In the course of the last twenty years the longings for a general appeasement have been especially pronounced in the consciousness of civilized nations. The preservation of peace has been put forward as the object of international policy; in its name, great States have concluded between themselves powerful alliances; it is the better to guarantee peace that they have developed, in proportions hitherto unprecedented, their military forces and still continue to increase them without shrinking from any sacrifice.

All these efforts, nevertheless, have not been able to bring about the beneficent results of the desired pacification. . . . . The intellectual and physical strength of the nations are for the major part diverted from their natural application, and unproductively consumed. Hundreds of millions are devoted to acquiring terrible engines of destruction which, though today regarded as the last word of science, are destined tomorrow to lose all value in consequence of some fresh discovery in the same field . . . . Moreover, the armaments . . . less and less fulfill the objects which the Governments have set themselves.

The economic crises, due in great part to the system of armaments *à l'outrance,* and the continued danger which lies in this massing of war material, are transforming the armed peace of our days into a crushing burden, which the peoples have more and more difficulty in bearing. It appears evident, then, that if this state of things were prolonged, *it would inevitably lead to the very cataclysm which it is desired to avert, and the horrors of which make every thinking man shudder in advance.*[10]

[10] James Brown Scott, *The Hague Peace Conferences of 1899 and 1907* (Johns Hopkins Press, 1909), II, 1–2. Italics added.

"To put an end to these incessant armaments" and to find means of "warding off calamities which are threatening the whole world" was, the Rescript concluded, "the supreme duty which is today imposed on all states." Three-quarters of a century later, it still is.

How the duty might be discharged, the Rescript did not attempt to specify; but after receiving the gingerly acceptance of the powers to this novel (and clearly dubious) invitation, the Russian Foreign Minister issued a circular proposing an agenda. This suggested that the nations might agree to a two-year "freeze" of existing military-force levels and budget appropriations; they might agree to a series of prohibitions (on the use of "any new kind of firearms" or "explosives," on the use of submarine torpedo boats, on the "throwing of projectiles or explosives of any kind from balloons") as a means of checking the technological arms race. Finally, as a kind of *lagniappe,* the Russians threw in a suggestion for the discussion of improved arbitral means for the peaceful settlement of international disputes. Thus provided with something concrete to work on, the press and foreign offices of the powers devoted themselves to demonstrating the utter impracticability of such notions, except possibly the innocuous last.[11] By the time the conference met

---

[11] One might have expected this sort of thing from the "bellicose" Germans. But the reaction of the "pacific" United States, then emerging from the Spanish-American War under the heady influence of victory, is instructive. Of course, we would gladly discuss proposals looking toward peaceful settlement of disputes. But, as the Secretary of State, John Hay, instructed our delegates, our own forces were already relatively so small that the proposed "freeze" of force levels was simply "inapplicable" to them; and he was unimpressed by the proposals looking toward a halt in

37

at The Hague in May, 1899, with Mr. Bloch himself hovering, unofficially, over every session, it was all over. Nothing of consequence was to emerge. The great problem of war and armaments had been fairly posed; and every argument that through the ensuing three-quarters of a century was to render its solution impossible had been fully developed. From The Hague in 1899 to Geneva in 1962 the dreary drama has been repeated, like a burlesque show in which the jokes are eternal, with only minor "topical" changes in the lines in which they are framed. Only, in this drama, the jokes are not very funny.

Still, the small fire of sense and reason—lighted, oddly enough, by the joint effort of the self-made Jewish business-man and the Czar of All the Russias—did not flicker out. More and more came to see the war problem as not only of the direst urgency but also as susceptible to solution. The Nobel Peace Prize was set up in 1901. Andrew Carnegie built the "peace palace" at The Hague to house the Permanent Court of International Arbitration, which had been one of the few concrete results of the 1899 conference. He also established the Carnegie Endowment for International Peace, with the optimistic proviso that once its object had been attained the

---

the technological arms race. "The expediency of restraining the inventive genius of our people in the direction of devising means of defense" was "by no means clear" to him (three-quarters of a century later the inexpediency of doing nothing in this area was less obscure), while, as he more soundly reasoned, no agreements in this area were likely to prove "effective" when the chips were down. He firmly enjoined the delegates against supporting any projects of this kind. Thus, at this interesting juncture of history, even the "pacific" and largely disinterested United States had nothing constructive to offer. *Op. cit.,* II, 7–8.

revenue was to be employed in furthering other causes of benefit to humanity. Bloch died in 1902, before the Russo-Japanese War had given its grim confirmation of many of his views about the nature of the new warfare, but his ideas did not die with him. The possibility of the peaceful settlement of international disputes through arbitral or judicial process attracted a great deal of attention in the first decades of the century, laying many of the foundations upon which (in the United States) the League to Enforce Peace and ultimately the League of Nations were to be erected. Norman Angell was following quite closely in Bloch's footsteps when in 1910 he published *The Great Illusion,* the famous demonstration that war no longer "paid." Boldly the introduction opened:

Each nation pleads that its armaments are purely for defense, but such a plea necessarily implies that other nations have some interest in attack. What is this interest or supposed interest?

The supposed interest has its origin in the universally accepted theory that military and political power give a nation commercial and social advantages, that the wealth and prosperity of the defenseless nation are at the mercy of stronger nations, who may be tempted by such defenselessness to commit aggression, so that each nation is compelled to protect itself against the possible cupidity of neighbors.

The author boldly challenges this universal theory and declares it to be based upon a pure optical illusion.

Angell, like Bloch, stressed the great economic and technical changes that were outmoding the war system:

The author urges that these little recognized facts, mainly the outcome of purely modern conditions . . . have rendered the problems of modern international politics profoundly and essentially different from the ancient; yet our ideas are still dominated by the principles and axioms and phraseology of the old.[12]

The book was a sensation when it appeared. Four years later it was swept away on a wave of scorn, as the outbreak of the First World War seemed to destroy the whole argument. In fact, the war was, of course, to provide a terrible confirmation of its validity.

The nineteenth century war system—representing a graft of the new technology and the new concepts of popular sovereignty upon eighteenth century ideas of international politics—had been digging its own grave at least since the American Civil War if not from the time of Napoleon. In August, 1914, it collapsed into it. The First, or Great, War (as it is still sometimes called) was the ineluctable consequence of the war system itself. No doubt the follies, greeds, and ambitions of nations and of individual soldiers and statesmen contributed to its coming. But basically it came because this was the only possible outcome for the system of threat, counterthreat, armament, counterarmament, and war to which the international politics of the Atlantic world had been committed.

[12] Norman Angell, *The Great Illusion* (Putnam, 1910), pp. vii and ix.

CHAPTER THREE

THE COLLAPSE
OF WAR

A GENERATION OF PUBLICISTS, POLEMICISTS, AND SERIOUS HIS-
torians was to devote itself to the search for the "causes" of
the First World War and to the apportionment of the
"guilt." But it had no "causes," and the whole of this immense
intellectual labor has scarcely improved upon the conclusion
of Sir Edward Grey, the British Foreign Minister at the time,
looking back upon his work in 1925:

> More than one true thing may be said about the causes of the
> war, but the statement that comprises most truth is that militarism
> and the armaments inseparable from it made war inevitable.
> Armaments were intended to produce a sense of security in each
> nation . . . What they really did was to produce fear in every-
> body. Fear causes suspicion and hatred.[1]

[1] *Twenty-Five Years, 1892–1916,* Viscount Grey of Fallodon (New York,
Frederick A. Stokes, 1925), II, 53.

The war had no causes other than the system out of which it grew; the tragedy lay in the fact that there was nothing in the ideas, the concepts, and institutions of the day to make possible its prevention. As Sir Edward also said:

On the Continent all the Great Powers . . . were thinking of war in terms of previous experience and of the latter half of the nineteenth century. We were alone in foreboding that war in the twentieth century would be unlike anything that preceded it. The abyss was not generally seen even when the governments came to the edge of it. . . . In a crisis people cannot change their settled view on general matters; they are too busy with the particulars of the moment.[2]

Viscount Grey's distinction between the militaristic Continent and the more enlightened British was scarcely valid; he was himself more deeply embayed in the nineteenth century than he afterwards realized, but his depiction of the process is convincing. Few thoughtful people in the summer of 1914 could have doubted that war had been transformed since 1870 and that if the great war came it would be a catastrophe of unpredictable proportions. The Great War, as David Starr Jordan had said in 1913, "will never come. Humanly speaking, it is impossible." If it did come, the New York *Times* observed as 1914 opened, it "would be a calamity too great for the world to endure." On the very eve of the crisis a French publicist quite accurately observed that "the causes of war are diminishing"; it was absurd that the armaments should nevertheless continue to pile up explo-

[2] *Op. cit.*, II, 32.

sively. All the more important colonial disputes had been settled by that time; none of the conventional issues of economic advantage, "population pressure," lust for territory, was active; what international differences remained seemed minor and appeared to no one in 1914 as valid cause for the slaughter of a generation of European youth in their settlement. The disaster, when it so suddenly exploded, seemed inexplicable. "The bloodiest war ever fought on earth," as the New York *Times* cried in its agony on the morning of August 2, 1914, "and *the least justified of all wars since man emerged from barbarism* has apparently begun." (Italics added.)

One may assign varying degrees of "guilt"—at any rate, of recklessness or irresponsibility—to the many actors involved, but the Great War itself was no man's doing. For a century the international system had been building up to just this result. The national state of the early twentieth century was a vastly more powerful, more wealthy, more closely knit, and better weaponed system of human organization than were the kingly states that had preceded it. For all its power and wealth, it had at the same time steadily lost the sense of security enjoyed by the more loosely organized and more numerous national units of the past. Surrounded by other states of comparable power and cohesion, it had more to fear than its predecessors at the same time that it had more to protect. It was tending to lose its freedom of action. Constructed out of the concomitant notions of popular nationalism and popular sovereignty, it had to take the populace and popular opinion into account—even in the great autocracies—and popular opinion could interpose many difficulties in the way of such rational compromises in foreign policy as had been possible to the absolute kings. Under the impact of the new politics and new technology, major war was becoming "impossible," or at least highly dangerous and unattractive, to the nation-state at the same time that it was being driven to pile up the armaments, to incite the popular nationalist enthusiasms, to build the political alliance systems that all seemed necessary to defense but that could only create an impasse from which there was no escape.

The military institutions of the seventeenth and eighteenth centuries had regulated the relations of the nation-states with a reasonable degree of efficiency, justice, and economy. But the ideas about war and diplomacy that had grown up around those institutions, surviving into the popular, technologically advanced societies of the twentieth century, could no longer discharge that function. In the forty years after 1871, diplomacy successfully surmounted one crisis after another without a major war, but always at the price of bringing closer the crisis that would prove insurmountable. When that crisis suddenly and unexpectedly arrived in the summer of 1914, it did not seem, at the beginning, much, if any, worse than many that had gone before. But the expedients had run out. There were no more balancing combinations to be made. No more judicious surrenders were practicable. A system rigidified by the efforts of the soldiers and statesmen to fortify the security of their own nations against every possible threat had lost its last resilience and had fractured under the strain. Policy had been all but paralyzed by military systems supposedly developed as instruments of policy. War had ceased to provide security for any nation, and had become only a deadly pitfall into which a whole generation of Europeans and many more besides were dragged uncomprehendingly.

The great war that it had been impossible, given the concepts of the times, to avert could not, once it had begun, be decided or stopped. All the staffs had looked forward to and planned for a relatively short war and quick decision—something on the model of the Franco-Prussian War, but on a larger scale. What they had actually managed to prepare, with their massive mobilization plans and enormously enhanced firepower, was Bloch's predicted "siege" and deadlock. As Barbara Tuchman has observed:

The Battle of the Marne was one of the decisive battles of the world not because it determined that Germany would ultimately lose or the Allies ultimately win the war but because it determined that the war would go on. . . . The nations were caught in a trap, a trap made during the first thirty days out of battles that failed to be decisive, a trap from which there was, *and has been,* no exit.[3]

In the 1914 compaigns the consumption of life and of ammunition had been on a wholly unexpected scale. In an older day the war might have run down in an exhaustion of money, men, and resources. The modern state was not so limited an engine. There was no more than a pause at the

[3] *The Guns of August* (New York: The Macmillan Company, 1962), p. 440. Italics added.

beginning of 1915 while huge new armies were raised and the civilian industrial potentials were mobilized to fill the "shell shortages" and meet the other insatiable demands of the new warfare. But decision still eluded them; the only result was to feed more hundreds of thousands of lives into the terrible "meat grinders" of the vast fronts. Through some three appalling years no device of strategy or tactics succeeded in breaking the Western trench stalemate. In the East, the war was less static, but it was if anything more costly in life, and proved equally incapable of producing decision.

Yet a war that could not be won could not be ended, either. Toward the end of 1916, as all the nations stood exhausted and stalemated after the frightful losses of Verdun and the Somme, the Isonzo and the Russian offensives, there was a moment of hope that peace might be negotiated. Everywhere, a continuation of these futile slaughters seemed more and more insensate. There were growing popular peace movements. In Britain, Lord Lansdowne suggested to the Asquith government that the possibilities of peace might be explored. President Wilson was pondering intervention to secure a "peace without victory." But it was as conceptually impossible to make peace in 1916 as it had been to preserve it in 1914.

The Germans, still generally holding the military advantage, were as anxious for peace as Wilson, but when they forestalled him with their own proposal for negotiations, the answering cries of rage and anguish from all the Allied capitals slammed the door shut for good. To the Allies, this underhanded "peace offensive" came only as an encouraging sign of German weakness. It was because they saw defeat ahead, the argument ran, that the criminal Germans were trying to secure by negotiation the ill-got gains one more great Allied effort would wrest from them. For both sides, the enemy had become criminal by definition. In order to nerve their masses to the sufferings that now fell upon the whole population, all the powers had found it necessary to implant this conviction. For over two years every device of propagandist emotion and distortion had been utilized to establish the enemy (not the war system itself) as the sole cause of all the agony and devastation. Total victory and punishment had become essential. How could one stultify the two years of bloody effort by settling for anything less? How could one face one's heroic war dead after such an admission that their sacrifices had after all been rather pointless? As Tuchman also says, "Men could not sustain a war of such magnitude and pain without hope—the hope that its very enormity would ensure that it could never happen again. . . . the hope that out of it all some good would accrue to mankind." [4] After so enormous an investment of blood and passion already put into the goal of victory, there was no way, within the conceptual framework of the times, to cut the losses. The only option was to send more good money after bad, which in this dreadful context meant to send hundreds of thousands more good lives after those already ruined or destroyed.

By the end of 1916 the Great War had lost all sense or meaning except as a naked struggle for power, in which the

[4] *Op. cit.,* p. 439.

uses to which the power might be put had all but disappeared under the ferocity of the struggle for its achievement. Woodrow Wilson did have a notion that the power, once acquired, could be employed to promote "the healing processes," to establish lasting peace, to demilitarize the world. But when on the heels of the German note, Wilson finally issued his own suggestion that the war might be negotiable, the reaction was well summarized by a leading British soldier: "That ass President Wilson has barged in and asked all belligerents their terms." [5] It was a pithy, if doubtless unintentional and unconscious, expression of a new fact in international society. War no longer had any terms, any aims. The endless talk about war aims, war objectives, the acquisition of territory or economic advantage, that has gone on ever since has been largely irrelevant. The only aim is an almost mystic concept of abstract power, for which "ignorant armies strive by night" with no notion of what can be done with the power once it is secured.

Victory was in the end achieved by Allied arms. Yet curiously enough it was not really military victory. It was revolution and collapse in Russia that gave Germany her success in the East in 1917–1918; it was ultimately mutiny and revolution at home that brought about her submission to the Western Allies in 1918. The armies might have gone on fighting to the end (as in large measure they did in 1945) without greatly affecting the vast political and social reorganizations that took place in 1917 and 1918. The armies could

[5] The soldier was Sir Henry Wilson. Quoted in Walter Millis, *Road to War* (Cambridge, Mass.: Houghton Mifflin, 1935), p. 368.

tear the world to pieces, but were of not much help in the reconstructions that necessarily had to follow. And the "power," won finally by the Allies at the cost of such oceans of blood and illimitable misery, was accompanied by no valid notion of what could be done with it.

The "Big Four" at Versailles (the United States, Britain, France, and Italy) disposed among them of a military power unchallengeable by any other national or political grouping in the world. Their conscious purpose was to employ this power in such a way as to render a repetition of the 1914 disaster impossible and to establish a permanent peace among nations. Their lamentable failure has been ascribed to many causes. Perhaps the most basic can be found in the fact that military power is not an instrument that can be applied—short of some global conquest like that which the *Pax Romana* imposed in antiquity—to the making or maintenance of peace.

The settlement failed in part because of the conflicting analyses of the peace problem and the conflicting national policies the victors brought to the Peace Conference. But each of the divergent policies was essentially military. All of them, even Wilson's, began with the assumption that the first requisite to peace was not the general abolition of the war system; it was the disarmament of Germany (the criminal in Allied definition) and the destruction of German "militarism." This disarmament and demilitarization could only (it seemed) be imposed by military force, which necessitated the maintenance, at least temporarily, of Allied armaments and Allied militarism. In the peace settlements, the disarmament of Germany was linked with an Allied undertaking to reduce their own armaments. But somehow, this never seemed possible. Allied disarmament proved no easier after the suppression of German militarism than it had proved before. Having founded the new peace on victorious armaments, the victors could not thereafter devalue their armed might. The war system—and all the myths and emotions surrounding it—which had made it impossible to avert the war in 1914, which had made it impossible to negotiate the struggle in 1916, made it impossible to make peace in 1919. In the result, no real peace was made.

It is almost inconceivable that the great peoples and their governments, standing amid all the passions, the hatreds, and the wreckage of 1919, could have made an enduring peace. Yet one cannot help speculating on what might have happened had the attempt been made. It would have had to have been a "peace without victory," as Wilson had told them all in 1916. It would have had to have accepted the world power structure substantially as the fighting had left it. Actually, the Fourteen Points (accepted by the Germans as a basis of negotiation) came close to doing this. Many of its terms were vague, but the specific territorial settlements proposed— evacuation of Belgium, restoration of Alsace-Lorraine, evacuation of Russia with acceptance of an independent Polish state having access to the sea—represented a rational balance of the outcome of all the fighting. The victors would have had to have been willing to take the vanquished into an equal partnership in the new world the war had made. For this, the demilitarization of Germany was of course essential, but so was the demilitarization of all the others—which constituted one of the Fourteen Points. The victors, in short, would have had to take the position that all had just barely emerged from a common disaster, of which no one state or statesman was primarily guilty but in which all had been about equally the victims of a useless and ruinous war system. They would have had to have taken the attitude that Germany, now disarmed and under a democratic form of government—the two conditions the Allies had made their principal war aims—would become a partner in the reconstruction of a disarmed and therefore permanent peace.

In 1919 such an attitude would have been impossible to the victors. They desperately wanted peace, but they had nothing in their political and emotional equipment that would enable them to *make* peace. Immediately, they were interested less in making peace than in using the overwhelming military power the dissolution of the German and Russian armies had apparently put into their hands in order to achieve still further victories—political and economic—which were to prove unattainable by military means. Even as the statesmen sat at Paris, the formidable military power they believed themselves to be wielding was slipping away from them not only in demobilization but also in the rise of vexing issues to which military power was inapplicable. A little later the French were to try to collect their reparations debts by occupying the Ruhr; they had the military force with which to occupy the Ruhr, but it turned out that war debts are not collectible in this way.

To make a real peace without victory was not *technically*

impossible in 1919, but it was humanly impossible. Men's governing ideas about the nature of international society, of war and of diplomacy, prevented it in 1919. What the world got was the peace of victory, which soon proved to be no peace at all. It was not merely that the great war armies demobilized; the real trouble was that the very large military forces that remained could not deal with the real issues with which they were confronted. A. J. P. Taylor has remarked that by destroying the German armies the Allies destroyed the only target against which their own armies could be launched. After Hitler had re-created the German Army there was something against which military "power" could be applied; before then, there was very little. The victors became hopelessly involved in Russia in 1919 and 1920, trying to produce with armed intervention political consequences that armies were incapable of delivering. Armies were not in the long run going to preserve Russia from Communism or save India for the British Raj or solve the complicated problems of the Near East and Palestine. Despite the postwar demobilizations, there was plenty of armed power available in the 1920's, but it could not stay the march of history—until the new militarisms arose to provide it with objectives.

The modern war system might well have been put out of business in 1919, but it was not. Mussolini and the Japanese militarists were the first to revive it in fact in order to confound the great powers who continued to cling to it tenaciously in theory. But it was Hitler who was finally to turn it against them to their own near destruction. Taylor, who has been called (perhaps not altogether justly) the first "revisionist" of the Second World War, has not tried to exculpate Hitler from his enormous crimes so much as to show that he was the product of a system that both invited and permitted those crimes. The Austrian corporal came out of the political slums of European international relations equipped with a switchblade knife of a singularly deadly character. Whose fault was it? Those who insisted on maintaining and trying to profit by the slums, or those who seized the criminal opportunities they offered? The question admits of no answer; one can only say that Hitler, an altogether "extraordinary" man, lusting for power and prominence in the postwar world, found in the *Diktat* of Versailles his most convenient instrument for their attainment. If the Allies had been capable of making peace in 1919, there could hardly have been a Hitler. What they actually made was a prolonged cold war on Germany. It was that war that enabled Hitler to rouse all the passions of nationalism and militarism the Allies had intended to extirpate, first to promote himself to power within Germany and then to convert the common disaster of the great depression into the basis for German rearmament and so to turn the Allies' war system—in their hands a useless and feeble instrument—against them with terrible effect. This is neither to condemn the Allies nor to justify the lawless and brutal men who took advantage of the Allies' misplaced confidence in their military power. It is simply to condemn a system—a system that, as it proved, was to profit the brutes and savages of statesmanship as little as it profited their generally more high-minded opponents.

For neither was it to prove an operable system for the conduct of international relations.

The miserable history of the thirties is a history of the *status quo* powers endeavoring to defend their status by the *threat* of military action that they dared not relinquish but that they feared increasingly actually to use; and of the insurgent powers rising to claim "dominance" by exploiting that reluctance. Again, it was a fairly naked struggle for abstract power, neither side making it at all clear what it would do with its power, once achieved, or, indeed, having any idea itself as to the positive uses to which actually it might be put. Most of Hitler's declared objectives—the acquisition of *lebensraum,* the reincorporation of the "racial Germans" in the body of the Reich, and so on—were what Ropp calls "bargaining and position papers," devices with which to seize power rather than specifications as to what would in fact be done with it. Hitler was the great "brinkman" of history. He probably never really "wanted" a great war, believing that he could enforce his power and dominance without one. But he was willing to gamble on the risk of major war. And France and Britain, who had after all determined the rules of this game of "power," found that all their great military power was paralyzed in its contexts. There were dozens of reasons, inherent in the nature of the military-political system, built up by the integrated, popular-technological state, why they could not forcibly prevent the reoccupation of the Rhineland, or German rearmament, or the Austrian *Anschluss,* or the ravishing of Spain (and of China); just as there were dozens of reasons, also inherent in the nature of the modern nation-state, why they could not divest themselves of an apparatus of military "power" that was increasingly powerless for either offense or defense in the new world.

The military problem—in itself insoluble by military means—was of course complicated by the fact that not two but three great parties were involved. Nazi Germany, Soviet Russia, and the Western democracies each saw in the other two major enemies and major threats to its own survival. Each sought to play the other two against each other in the interests of its own defense and dominance. Even less was this a situation that could be resolved by military action or even by the threat of military power. It offered no foundation for a more rational world order based ultimately upon war. It was a situation that could be exploited—up to a point —by a "brinkman" gambling for power in the abstract. Hitler was by far the best, the most iron-nerved, gambler in the lot, and each gamble paid off better than the previous one until the last—in August, 1939, when his hand was finally called. By skillful exploitation of the European war system, he had climbed to an undeniable "predominance" in Europe without resort to war. In August, 1939, Hitler was surely the most "powerful" statesman and Germany the most "powerful" state in the Western world. But having done it all by the threat of war, when the Poles at that point refused to throw in their hand he had to go to war. He was, of course, to achieve tremendous military successes thereafter. But from that point on, his real power—his effective power to mold world society or even the German future in it—began its steady decline, until four and a half years later it had so contracted that the only "power" left him was the power to kill his mistress and himself.

The war system turned out to be no more practicable or operable for those who sought to exploit it for the advancement of their "power" than for those who sought to shelter behind it in defense of their own. It is not difficult to see in retrospect that it was only while they could "credibly" threaten major war that the Japanese, Mussolini, and Hitler were powerful in fact; it was with their actual resort to war that their power to control events began to evaporate. And while their great opponents, by their answering resort to war, were able to avert defeat, they were still not able to utilize their vast military might for the construction of a world tolerable to themselves—or to anyone else. Their famous policy of "unconditional surrender" (it was announced at Casablanca at the end of 1942, but had been implicit from the beginning) arose out of the fact that there was no more positive policy on which there was any chance that the three major partners could agree. It was really 1916 all over again. In 1942 there was no "ass," like President Wilson, to "barge in" and ask for war aims; but there were no war aims. The only object a war of this character could have was the object—in itself totally barren—of victory, without reference to its uses. The war leaders—Roosevelt, Churchill, and Stalin—were all prisoners even more than manipulators of the system that enmeshed them. Only long after Germany had, for a second time, been totally defeated and disarmed did the lineaments of a new and more workable world system begin to appear. The peace the victors of 1918 might have made with the Weimar Republic was finally made with Adenauer's—but it was not made by the armies and it was not made at all until some ten or fifteen years after the fighting had ceased.

The new world system has appeared as yet in only rudimentary form. Even so, its really basic institutional beginnings are not the creation of the Second War armies, and few of them could even have been foreseen in the hour of "victory" in 1945. The Western peace with West Germany, German rearmament, NATO, the Warsaw Pact, the European Common Market, the Coal and Steel Community, the Organization of American States, the restoration of Japan as a power in the Asian balance, the unification of China, all would have seemed improbable—and most of them inconceivable—as "victory" impended in the spring of 1945. The greatest of all wars had failed to produce, or even to sketch the design of, the actual institutional structure that in the subsequent decade and a half appeared to be essential to human survival and progress.

It is difficult to imagine a clearer demonstration of the inutility of the modern war system—for defenders and revolutionaries alike—than that provided by the thirty years of agonized history between 1914 and 1945. To the end of the eighteenth century war was as normal, if costly and disagreeable, a part of political life as disease was of private life. But after the Napoleonic Wars people began to say (as Goya, for one, did in his terrible drawings) that this kind of thing was as impossible as it was inhuman. Many more said it after the American Civil War; millions said it after 1918—in the aftermath of "the war to end war." After 1945 the mood was more sober, more sophisticated but more baffled. Major war was obviously even more "impossible" than in the past; but all suggested means of coping with it had been cruelly defeated. The League of Nations had proved a failure. Disarmament was apparently unattainable. Most of the major powers were left in a bitter resolve to maintain their weapons systems, but only as a "deterrent" to what all past history had indicated was not deterrable by military means.

It is ironic—though perhaps it was inevitable, given the history of modern technology—that in the very last days of this second war to end war, there appeared the atomic bomb. At the moment in which war was becoming most obviously useless, a genuine deterrent had for the first time been made available to man—in the form of military power raised to so dreadful a magnitude as to be unusable in either war or politics. The abolition of war had become a possibility. Yet there was a tragic duality of effect. In producing the means through which war might be abolished, the nuclear weaponry also produced what seemed to be a way in which the war system could be maintained.

In 1945 the armies, fleets, and conventionally armed air forces had really fought themselves to a standstill. As the careful postwar studies of the United States Strategic Bombing Survey showed, the appearance of "air power," proclaimed by its advocates as the means of breaking the strategic-technological deadlock and restoring the power of decision to military action, had failed to fulfill the promise.

With nothing more than TNT bombs, it could enormously enhance the random savagery and destruction of war but without producing corresponding military effect. Considering the bloody futilities of 1939–1945, a general disarmament in the aftermath of the war is at least not inconceivable. But at Hiroshima "air power" had suddenly been presented with a weapon that was surely decisive—"absolute," as we were inclined to call it in our first enthusiasm—and the war system had apparently been preserved. In the brief period of the American monopoly there were not a few who seized upon the colossal bombs as at last providing the means through which we could dictate peace. But peace cannot be dictated, and certainly cannot be dictated by military means. All that the new weapons succeeded in dictating was the Soviet development of a nuclear arsenal of its own.

It was to take over fifteen painful years for some dawning realization of what this implied to appear. Some rudiments of a warless international politics and power structure have grown gradually out of the "cold war." Over fifteen years after Hiroshima we find the heads of the world's two most powerful military states formally and officially committed to the "general and complete disarmament" Hiroshima made ultimately inevitable. Yet, enmeshed as they are in the concepts of the war system, neither has known how to make any progress toward that goal.

Military power remained the only imaginable basis for the international society just as it was becoming in itself unusable, and was doomed to become only the more unusable, the greater the heights of terror to which the new arms race might build it. World statesmanship knows that humanity faces a clear choice between demilitarization or destruction, but it does not know how the choice is to be made. This is the dilemma that has confronted us all for the past fifteen years, and in face of which so much anguished thought has been poured out over possible strategies, over "deterrence" and "limited war," over techniques for "arms control," as well as over attempts to save the military foundations of the world society through the superficially political devices of international authority and "world law." All attempts to establish peace while retaining the war system have so far failed. They have brought us to the grim present position as described in the ensuing chapter.

CHAPTER FOUR

THE PRESENT PREDICAMENT

THE PRECEDING CHAPTERS HAVE DEALT WITH SOME OF THE aspects of the history of modern warfare and the political and social forces that drove it on as the overwhelming terminal instrument of legal and extralegal society. We find ourselves at the point in time where the arts and sciences of war have so clearly outstripped all other technological development in the world as to render the system useless for its traditional role.

History has been drawn upon in the realization that it is not itself an absolute art. Historians skew and dilute the records of the past in accordance with their own predilections and actions, and thus further muddy already opaque waters. It is even more difficult to attempt to evaluate the present. Not only is a large portion of the "record" hidden from us, but even when it is available (and in spite of the marvels of modern machine information gathering and collation) we see the same proclivities in those who supply it consciously or unconsciously to tamper with and color the raw material from which understanding must come. Discrimination, the principal task of the people attempting to evaluate modern military, political, and social systems, is made daily more difficult because of the volume and velocity of the great masses of data that make up the symbols of world activity. We know that much of it is unreliable, but we do not know which of it is—or how much.

It is a truism that no man is any longer an expert in any even moderately technical subject. Once he moves outside his restricted portion of a single field of science or technology, he is quickly in difficulty. And should he attempt to apply a second, third, and fourth area of expertise to his own small store of real knowledge, his problems of understanding and communication magnify unbearably. As one consequence, many writers on modern strategy and twentieth century war are persons who carry the most credibility with the most people—those whose daily work, however narrow in scope, is so widely recognized as being intellectually difficult that they are *believed* to know almost everything about anything less difficult. During the last few years these authors have been the "hard" scientists, mostly mathematicians and physicists, with a sprinkling of the practitioners of lesser known arts. It is not hard to see why this should be so. Everyone is convinced of the almost unmanageable complexity of the modern world of social, political, and economic forces that are all entwined in the mammoth war machines. Politicians, presidents, kings, and dictators have erred so often, so dramatically, and (thanks to the proliferation of mass communications) so publicly, that the people's mistrust of leadership in the traditional sense has finally evinced itself in this new dependence on the group most widely thought to possess the greatest capacity for fact-gathering and problem-solving in the classic scientific sense.

What is not widely perceived is that although these men do indeed have a superior capacity for orderly correlation and conclusion compared to the intellectual struggles of most men, this advantage is not overwhelming simply because of the volume and scope of information and understanding necessary for any reasonably *total* assessment of the problems and consequences of modern nuclear conflict. Wide disparities of opinion between and among these gifted men when dealing with these subjects are well known and highly publicized. Everyone from the Joint Chiefs of Staff to local Chambers of Commerce is subjected to positivisms that cruelly mock what used to be meant by the "scientific method." Most of the time these scientists have difficulty admitting what each of them knows—that speculations about the probabilities and the effects of thermonuclear war cannot be put forward with any reasonable degree of certitude. The forces involved are quite unimaginable, and they are just about as unimaginable to the most sophisticated physicist as they are to anyone else. All these speculations are grounded on not very sophisticated calculations and guesses that produce such simplified prognostications as the "saving of 90 percent of the American people," or, conversely, "the destruction of 90 percent of the American people." Both conclusions are specious. Yet calculations of this sort have led us to the thesis of stable deterrence and, at the same time, to the negation of this same system by the endorsement of a vast national shelter program.

The reason for our inability to understand even part of our present predicament is primarily this: We have no body of practical evidence upon which to base projections of the kind we now find are too often the thin spine of national and international policy. In trying to describe the forces involved in modern weapons, for example, one is reduced to simple kinds of arithmetical devices that attempt to describe things that have never happened. We could belabor the old example of the World War II bomber by trying to imagine the simultaneous unleashing of the high-explosive load of an incomprehensible one million bombers as the equivalent of only one 100-megaton explosion. But since not even one-tenth of a million bombers have ever been built, let alone brought into the same space at the same time, the analogy comes to very nearly nothing.

None of the innumerable examples of the power for devastation of modern weaponry is really believable. They are not believable for the simple reason that this kind of power and its effects have never been demonstrated.

For the first time in history, we do not know what military power really consists of. Although there have been some immense miscalculations of the utility and power of pre-atomic weaponry, there has always been some practical basis for reasonable calculations from the projection of past experience. For example, the United States Strategic Bombing Survey of Germany, made in 1945, revealed that the Allies had grossly miscalculated the ability of the German war machine to continue to operate. Yet, there was not much new that was revealed about the force, singly or cumulatively, of the two-ton blockbuster. Within reasonable limits, the weapon almost invariably did what it was predicted that it would do. What went wrong with the calculations was quite aside from the actual "pure" effects of the weapons themselves. We failed to assess accurately the ability of the Nazi high command to keep the people at work; we neglected to think very hard about techniques of dispersal and cover that were then unorthodox; and, finally, we were quite unaware of the surprising inability of Allied bomber crews to hit what they were trying to hit. People argued then and will continue to argue about the strategic and tactical mistakes made in the delivery methods and target selection decided upon during this period, but few have any serious questions about the predicted *force* of the bombs when they finally exploded.

Scientists usually like to make clear the line between projection and prediction. They are fond of projection. They allege that they avoid prediction at all cost. Yet, within the last five years we have been subjected to an orgy of prediction based on the most feeble and fragmentary theoretical calculations.

Projecting the effects of the explosion of 20 or 100 megatons over a modern, living city rests entirely upon the calculations extrapolated from much smaller explosions and really measures in the crudest ways only the massive physical forces involved—blast, shock, fire, radiation, and fallout. Trying to predict from these skimpy data what would happen to the people, their artifacts, and their environment is much like trying to imagine a B-70 from careful scrutiny of a chickadee in flight. Recognition of our incapacity to know what we have in thermonuclear force and what its effects might be is occasionally seen in additions to the jargon of the operations analysts of such terms as D.O.E.—death of earth. Death of earth simply means that some percentage of the face of the globe is so blasted, burned, and contaminated that no living thing remains on it or near it, nor can any valid predictions be made as to when it can support any sort of life—if ever. No one anywhere, no matter how erudite or experienced, has any way to envisage the physical and psychological damage to a population under this kind of attack; what will happen to the fabric of the society; whether a quiescent, shocked, primitive band of survivors could emerge with a reasonable chance to restore the modern world to some semblance of what we now have or whether there might take place a phenomenon that is almost unimaginable—that of a shattered, completely psychotic population.

One does not have to deal with the enormities of a thermonuclear war to illustrate the recent failures of the best of the world's scientific population to foresee developments even in their own fields. For example, in 1937, under the aegis of the American Academy of Sciences, a distinguished group of scientists was assigned the task of predicting the major inventions that would affect the course of human events in the succeeding ten-year period. Among the items overlooked by this very capable group were many things in development at the time. Great advances in medicine were predicted, but antibiotics were overlooked. The speed of propeller-driven aircraft was foreseen as trebling, yet the possibility of the perfection of the jet engine was not mentioned. Even radar, which was to be the salvation of beleaguered England four years later, was not foreseen by the group. It is doubtful that our abilities to perceive cumulative effects of weapons of current force or the intervening inventions that will raise their power to even greater heights is any more developed now than it was in the years of the last great war. Thus, a detailed assessment of the way things are wobbles on the flimsy hinges of our scant ability to assess what we have, and a dismal historical record for projecting things as they might be tomorrow.

A distinguished British scientist, Sir Solly Zuckerman, writing from material he contributed to a symposium on "Science and Warfare in the 1970's," [1] reflects the doubts of an experienced operations analyst about the competence of the "game theorist" to tamper with the vagaries of reality by translations into logical symbolism:

What worries me is the fact that the total situation with which the theorists deal also contains extremely broad parameters of so qualitative a nature that no one could attribute numerical values to them. Some of these parameters are among the most important. For example, they include such matters as the enemy's intentions, as well as his strength and capacity; the resolution of our people;

[1] Sir Solly Zuckerman, "Judgment and Control in Modern Warfare," *Foreign Affairs*, January, 1962.

the capacity of a country to restore itself economically when it has suffered a degree of devastation well beyond anything that lives within human comprehension—let alone experience—and other matters equally vague. These are vitally important issues. But they are not numerical issues, and probably never can be made such, even if they were ever to come within our experience.

Much has been written about the probable effects of a massive thermonuclear exchange between two great powers. There really seems not much more to be said on the subject. We know by relatively simple calculations that both the Soviet Union and the United States have the capability to destroy either continental mass many times over. We know that the current riposte to this inconceivable state of affairs is that we shall continue to manufacture greater and more efficient means to "overkill" each other unless there is rational intervention of a kind no one seems able to imagine. But although we might not yet know how to stop the engines of destruction nor how to stop their manufacture nor how to dismantle completely or partially the juggernaut of thermonuclear war, we can make some observations upon critical changes in social and moral attitudes that have permitted the accumulation of this power for mutual suicide.

Erich Kahler[2] has commented at length upon a grisly phenomenon he calls "unique to the epoch," which sprang up and was sustained in Nazi Germany during World War II— a unique schizoid behavior of the people who created and maintained the German war machine. He comments not

[2] Erich Kahler, *The Tower and the Abyss* (New York: George Braziller, Inc., 1957).

only on the incredible ability of the soldier to divorce all human feeling from his chores as torturer and executioner but also on the pervasive quality of this horrifying detachment from experience and teaching by so many thousands of Germans who served the war machine in more remote ways. He points particularly to the management of the Krupp, Siemens, and I. G. Farben corporations, which utilized slave labor under the most inhuman conditions and whose executives were able at the end of the day to resume the placid life of upper-middle-class *Herrenvolk* without the slightest intrusion of guilt or self-incrimination. Kahler asks:

What it it then, that we may regard as new in these happenings? The fateful novelty may be seen, I believe, in that accomplished split in the personality, a split reaching deep enough to shatter the identity of the human being. Those persons, Elite Guards, intellectuals, executives, whom we have seen professionally attending to the most gruesome activities, seem to act with only a certain part of their being, while another part was left behind, remained in the background; in fact, their behavior bears a resemblance to technological procedures and can best be expressed in technological terms. We could say that different faculties of the human being are switched off or turned on according to requirement; and substantially, these different faculties, or sections of the personality seem entirely disconnected from one another.

It may be that a similar acceptance of "the way things are" has quietly eroded the consciences and sensibilities of modern man. It might be argued that the dazzling development of the technological age, from automobiles to missiles, has similarly fractionated the attitudes and unconscious behavior of all of us living in a world overwhelmed with these objects. One of the insidious qualities of the machines themselves is that they can almost always be eloquently defended by Russians, Americans, or Chinese as either absolutely necessary or, at the very least, useful. To note a relatively minor example, it is difficult to argue that mobile America does not depend upon the automobile. The fact that its proliferation has stultified the development of more rational means of transportation in the metropolitan areas, and has led to the deep sickness and imminent demise of almost every other form of transportation except for air, must be overlooked if on no other ground than that the industry itself exists—is so vital to the economic well-being of the country that a poor year in the industry can literally set off a major depression in the United States.

Although some attention has been given in the last few years to the nature of the ultimate, predictable self-defeat of their users by the tens of millions of cars that are to be manufactured within the next few years, little serious support for getting at the problem itself has come forward. It is not that planners for the gigantic metropolitan constellations we see for the 1970's are not able to envisage more rational ways of getting about than assigning two tons of steel and high-priced, fantastically inefficient machinery to each 150 pounds of human being. They can and they have. But theirs is a lost cause. The matter is already out of hand, and has no tendency whatever to reverse itself. America on wheels will become progressively more intolerable because we do not seem to have any idea as to methods of control over things (and the industries that make them) that afford a short-term pleasure, right, or profit, either for us as individuals or for the formidable organizations formed and maintained to protect and forward the manufacture and ownership of the paraphernalia, even when the insistence upon the continuation of the system so clearly presages crisis in the society it was designed to benefit. The fact that automobile fatalities in Los Angeles County in 1961 exceeded the United States Marines' losses at Tarawa and that its metropolitan area is now 27 percent paved for the dubious and inadequate accommodation of the present accumulation of motor vehicles has impelled no rational preparation for the projected doubling of the number of passenger vehicles to be dumped into that area over the next fifteen-year period.

In a much more lethal but nevertheless similar way the technological advance of weaponry has insulated its makers and potential users from seriously considering anything but a further perfection of these deadly machines and a relentless drive toward accumulating more of them in more "sophisticated" forms. On every side we see intellectual and emotional accommodations being made to the mechanics and probable effects of World War III. A harrowing philosophical change is slowly being made by the people here and abroad in their attitudes toward these going institutions. We have witnessed the inch-by-inch retreat of many Western scientists in their views of the usefulness and practicability of catastrophic warmaking gadgetry since the initial revulsion by so many of them to the horrors of Hiroshima and Nagasaki. One reason may be that there are now third- and fourth-generation scientists and engineers who have never been employed in any capacity other than that of attending to the war machine. Their acceptance of their lives as paramilitary is in most cases complete and accommodated with relative ease. Aside from the salubrious effects of high compensation and generally pleasant working environments, the game has come to be for the sake of the game—*pour le sport* —an entrancing, highly competitive career wholly devoted to the eventual annihilation of all human existence. Just as in the case of the hundreds of thousands of individuals engaged in the design, production, selling, and maintenance of the auto, there seems to be no other conceivable way of life to which either they or their leaders have given much serious attention.

Out of this group have come the elite, scientific segment generally called "operations analysts." It is in listening to their words that we come by an inkling of the immense retreat of the scientists from their traditional positions as humanists and truth seekers. It is from these men we have learned the vocabulary of dispassionate terror: Death of Earth, overkill, megabuck, megadeath, thermal effects, tolerable death rate, and so on. They know perfectly well that what they are talking about is the violent deaths of millions of reasonably innocent human beings, and yet enough time has gone by since the establishment of the current modes of mass destruction that a schizoid manifestation similar to that noted by Kahler may be suggested.

The game is now clearly being played for its own sake— divorced from its inevitable consequences. This amazing separation of personality, which permits millions of scientists, technologists, military men, politicians, and supporting workers of many nations to spend their lives, planning, designing, and manufacturing the means to incinerate people precisely like themselves and, at the same time, act in their personal lives the roles requiring love and charity, or at least decency, without ever a backward glance at the colossus they have made and are elaborating is a phenomenon that promises little for the future of the earth. Any of these men would seethe with indignation at being compared to the German scientists, medical men, and industrialists who helped bring such immeasurable suffering to so many millions of people in World War II. Yet, is not the major difference only that the carnage has not yet begun? Along with its blessings, technology seems to have produced a unique virus, one that suppresses humanitarian instincts, that mesmerizes its victims with the mechanics of death, and that, like any sturdy virus, knows no national boundaries.

Since all these activities and their results are in all countries blessed with the impeccable label of Defense, there seems slim hope at this time that the worldwide weapons business will get anything but slicker and larger and that its practitioners will become even more inured to what they are really about, which is the application of their incredible pool of talent, not to ways out of the dilemma of a war system long ago demonstrated to be obsolete, but to the steady perfection of the fascinating gadgetry of the twentieth century war apparatus.

Thus, it can be argued that the mesmeric novelty of the

thermonuclear war machines, beyond complete understanding by anyone, let alone a significant proportion of the population, has diverted attention from the subtle and profound accommodations in our social, political, and economic systems that will arise out of maintaining and forwarding the gigantic congeries of organization and apparatus both we and the Russians have come to call "defense." Men everywhere have been so bemused by the wonders of missiles that are as high as a fourteen-story building, by computers which we have been taught to believe "think"—in short, by heroics on a level far beyond anything that can reasonably be grasped, that the future of the major powers and of the rest of the world seems inextricably bound to our engines of obliteration. There seems to be a perverse and macabre "pride of ownership" (as the automobile people put it) in possessing enough destructive power to obliterate the world several times over [3]—especially when the weapons and the gear attached to them elicit wonder and awe from every one of us who has ever admired a handsome, functional mechanical object. Indeed, preoccupation with airborne weaponry and its subsidiary objective, space penetration, has become America's and Russia's leading spectator sport.

[3] At present weapon-program rates, we shall within the next six years elevate our annihilatory capacity by at least another 60 percent. Thus, in 1968 we are promised the possession by the U.S. alone of the equivalent of 105 billion tons of TNT, about 35 tons per human being. If one doubles this number to account for the nuclear holdings then projected for the non-U.S. orbit, each of us then on earth will be honored by the existence of more explosive dedicated to our personal containment than was used to excavate for Hoover Dam.

Thus dazzled, it is difficult to imagine the opposite state of affairs—that of not possessing this glamorous inventory of lethal gadgetry. But we should try to disengage ourselves from our fascination with the present system in order to try to see what we must pay to keep it. Impressive as the costs of mounting the twentieth century war machine have already been, the social, political, and economic systems of our own and all other major nations must continue to be warped and accommodated to the seemingly limitless demands of the technology of mass destruction.

What is meant by the "demands" of war technology upon the United States for the next decade? An answer might be hazarded along these lines: In addition to the equipages necessary for a maximum "conventional" war such as World War II, an equal or greater expenditure of monies and effort must be directed to the delivery, support, and countermeasure systems required for the present and future thermonuclear arsenals.

What might this commitment mean in terms of dollars alone?

During the period 1951-1961 the defense budget more than doubled. Over one-fourth of all capital goods produced in the United States today is military hardware. Yet, in 1961 we were spending less dollars on all military expenditures than the $50 billion outlay in 1953—the height of the Korean War. Some economists concerned with military-budget projections look for only a gradual rise to the 1953 level by 1970 —a slow fiscal curve accounting for a $5-6 billion gain over a nine-year period.[4] Several assumptions are made in reaching this conclusion—that "the present state of international tension will continue, that there will be no 'fringe' wars, and that a workable disarmament program will not be adopted during the decade."[5] Of these controlling assumptions, only the last seems likely to prove correct. Although the "present state" of mutual suspicion and hostility between the United States and the USSR might remain relatively steady in its intensity throughout the decade, the slow addition of hostile powers to our growing list of "enemies" can increase the *total* state of tension greatly.

Almost every knowledgeable military student predicts the joining to the nuclear "club" of from three to ten nations during the next ten years. While several of these powers are either traditional allies of the United States or are neutrals (that is, Switzerland, Sweden, Belgium), the history of the military-political pressures and queasy international allegiances over the past ten years gives us little assurance that the persistent Soviet blackmail tactics will not erode even the most staunch of the smaller nations. Such eventualities would call for appropriate expansion of American military power to "cover" the gaps in the evacuated European defense system, and to provide for the contingency, however remote, of greatly increased aggressive thermonuclear positions toward us in the future.

If we add to these not inconceivable threats, the likelihood

[4] M. L. Weidenbaum, Corporate Economist, Boeing Airplane Co., "Defense Spending in the 1960's," American Management Association Report No. 57, 1961.

[5] *Op. cit.*

of powers now openly hostile to us acquiring for themselves the bomb and the means of delivering it, it is doubtful that gentle projections that involve the maintenance of the *status quo* are likely to be valid in 1970. If we were to be called upon either to fight or to seriously prepare for a war of the Korean dimension, or a combination of smaller engagements that added to the same thing, at least $25 billion per year would go into "conventional" arms and the manpower required to fight them. At the same time, we can expect the reserve thermonuclear force, the missiles, ground electronics, and aircraft directly engaged in nuclear delivery, which account at present for about 60 percent of the total military budget, to continue at about that level. This combination of circumstances might well accelerate our outlay for the combination war-and-defense system to $80–$100 billion per year. This more generous estimate has its advocates. Henry Rowan, in a 1960 study paper for the Joint Economic Committee of Congress,[6] sees no serious impediment to adding to the defense budget at the rate of $10 billion per year, provided the Gross National Product advance at the rather modest rate of 3 percent per annum. (In a footnote, Mr. Rowan himself used the word "modest" in reference to the "impact of a $10 or $15 billion increase in the national security budget. . . .") "Larger increases," he writes, "raise some questions about controls." If history is any guide, we shall probably elect to "overkill" with our fiscal weaponry, too.

It is no longer appropriate to separate expenditures for

[6] Henry Rowan, "National Security and the American Economy in the 1960's" (United States Government Printing Office, January 30, 1960).

weapons installations and fighting manpower from the sheltering of civilians and critical goods from enemy action. "Civil" defense is no longer an amateur affair, as we can now see from the shift of responsibility for its planning and execution to the Department of Defense. It is clear that civil protection is no longer solely a matter of self-preservation and humanitarian behavior, but is also a vital requirement of a first-rate war machine, necessary to the day-to-day brinkmanship we have been taught to call "credible" threat and counterthreat. This is military logic. If one can accept the idea that a terminal thermonuclear war is the only way to resolve political problems, it is probably pretty *good* military logic. But for some reason the American people quietly rejected the invitation to proceed with the elementary sandbagging of their persons. This lack of response has been variously attributed to lethargy and ignorance. Yet, it is just as probable that there is, in this country, a widespread (if unspoken) understanding that an "adequate" shelter system is an integral component of the war system and that contributing to the perfection of this system heightens the likelihood of its use. If purely military logic wins out in the end, each American, no matter how remote from the scene of actual military activity, must learn to bob into and out of his shelter with the same alacrity and certainty that we hope for from our nonhuman weapons. Although the initial federal budget for the civil defense program was minuscule—less than a billion dollars—one can speculate about where it is logically to go. We might use as a model the history of protection for intercontinental missiles. In the beginning, it seemed adequate to mount these new weapons much as coast artillery has always been deployed—in what amounted to a concrete-lined ditch. As the power of warheads and the accuracy of delivery systems improved, these early housings were termed "soft," that is, of no use in any situation other than one of first-strike. Since we were and are committed to "massive retaliation," it became obvious that "hard" bases— concrete and steel silos and the complicated tunnels and service equipment built to resist at least 100 pound psi of blast—would need to be installed. Other techniques of mobility and evasion, such as the rail-based Minuteman and seaborne Polaris, were either brought to a high state of development or actually put into operation, but the spine of the ICBM delivery system remains the deeply sheltered twentieth century fortresses, such as the squadrons being installed around Cheyenne, Wyoming, and Tucson, Arizona. If strictly military reasoning prevails, a similar sequence of events in the sheltering of human beings and their basic necessities seems the only logical outcome. The makeshift designs lately urged upon the population would prove to be only the first phase of a gradual "hardening" process. (If we are indeed thinking of 1970!) Even as the "hole and sandbag" program crept into being, public officials were exploring the feasibility of larger, permanent mass shelters near schools, parks, and centers of business and industry. The Los Angeles County Board of Supervisors has discussed the construction of enough of these underground structures to protect the 6 million human beings within its jurisdiction. The best estimate of cost at this writing is $100 per head, or $600 million for one metropolitan area alone. (The RAND Corporation's model hard-rock shelter system for Manhattan probably comes closer to fiscal reality at $500–$700 per occupant for 4 million persons.)

Inadequate as these designs will turn out to be, they are actually only a start. Vast stores of water, food, medicine —essential equipment of all kinds—must be purchased and stored. And if the underground concept is to be carried to its logical conclusion, one must provide for the instruments of recovery—machinery, fuel, and building materials, as well as the millions of items those doing the planning will think absolutely necessary to recovery.

Where this flight into the ground will lead depends upon the belief of the people that a thermonuclear war is probable. Once the notion of protection is widely held and believed, there are none but practical financial limits to the elaborations of the survival system.

It must occur to the proponents of the shelter system that a shrewd nuclear strategist may well "mix" his attack, in terms of weapon sizes and yield, air and ground bursts, and, perhaps most important, by withholding an unknown reserve of attack capability in order to strike a number of times in the same or different areas *after* the initial missile launch. If an attacker can maintain reserve nuclear firepower, there is every reason to suppose that when what remains of the population finally emerges from cover it will face a second, and perhaps a third, strike. When this probability is recognized, much more elaborate plans and structures will have to get under way than are now contemplated. The surviving population may face the prospects of months underground before the most rudimentary recovery efforts can begin. An adequate nationwide scheme to meet these conditions reduces the proposals advanced thus far to insignificance. Indeed, it is difficult to pursue the matter of financial outlay much beyond this point of conjecture. P. M. S. Blackett [7] points out, "As no large-scale nuclear war has ever occurred, there is no body of operational data on real events upon which to base a common-sense analysis. . . ." While Blackett was commenting on the analytic methods employed by some of the "academic military theorists" in the burgeoning literature of military speculation, his remark has pertinence to the matter at hand—the newly revealed recognition that the shelter program is an integral part of the military system. There is quite literally no predictable end to the erection of the "ultimate fortress," because there is no end to the savage power of weapons to come—the N bomb, the Y bomb, the Z bomb, and their capacities to wrench even the most elaborately defended and hidden population out of the depths of the earth and to fry them as surely as if they had been sitting in their homes.

President Kennedy has described our major military goal as "nuclear capacity second to none." If this is to be so, we should speculate as to whether or not it is achievable and, if so, at what cost. In doing so, we should regard the relative postures, techniques and capabilities of the two great powers from a purely military viewpoint, eschewing all apologies

[7] P. M. S. Blackett, "Critique of Some Contemporary Defense Thinking." *Encounter*, April, 1961.

for tradition, fair play, the American Way, and the rest of our nationalistic shibboleths. The objectives must be: Either to contain the present and future nuclear powers forevermore, so that no one will ever shoot at us, or, since this seems increasingly unlikely, to "win" a nuclear war fought with one or any combination of nuclear-equipped enemies.

The United States is publicly committed to a defensive, or so-called "second strike," policy. It might well be argued that the Soviets are similarly committed, but few Americans believe it. Since the position of the second-strike power is generally regarded as inferior to that of the aggressor, and if true "balance of terror" is what we are after, the first requirement in this exercise is that we release ourselves from this policy and make our consequent stance believable to the Russians. In order to do so, two important developments must occur. Reliable ICBM capability has to be achieved that will let us finally dispose of the manned bomber. Elaborate measures must be taken to shelter the civilian population.

Even though millions will die in any calculated missile exchange, civil defense is an integral component of the believable military threat, for an exposed people renders its own threat of attack hopelessly incredible.

We are now attempting to satisfy both of these requirements. Weaponry is slowly acquiring a semblance of reliability and the pressures for a vast shelter program are increasing. Although both requirements will take at least five years (and even then "reliability" will be a relative term), by 1967 we should be able, if we choose, seriously to reexamine the desirability of hitting the USSR first and, perhaps, launching a simultaneous preventive strike against China.

Other military requirements for the satisfactory parity-for-containment might include these:

1. Increase surveillance. Although Samos and similar very-high-altitude espionage devices may be a partial answer, they will be vulnerable to antisatellite devices that are bound to emerge in the next few years. We need not only a vastly expanded intelligence network (along more conventional lines) but also an acknowledged change of attitude and policy that would allow the use of infiltration techniques on a scale now employed by the Soviets. In short, Americans must admit to the necessity of spying—with all its gamy concomitants.

2. A consolidated military machine that would truly provide for the best "mix" of nuclear and conventional weapons use. Such makeshift conciliations as the old ground rule that Army missile responsibility was limited to one hundred miles, while all more distant ventures are in the province of the Air Force, is an example of the sacrifice of manageability of twentieth century war to the vanities of the nineteenth century institutions upon which we rely to fight it.

3. The building of vast underground shelter-cities to house and protect that part of the civilian population (perhaps 50 percent) we could have some hope of saving, as well as reserve foodstuffs, essential services, and manufacturing capacity with which to start the attempt to recover and rebuild. People who have thought about this staggering venture advance cost estimates in the $200–300 billion range.

The planning and construction time is estimated (on a crash basis) at from 5 to 13 years. All surface construction would have to cease, since the whole of the American construction and construction material industries would concentrate on the building of this vital adjunct to the war machine.

4. A controlled economy. To implement the necessary projects for parity, the budget for arms and civilian protection should increase sharply, beginning immediately. By 1965 this portion of the federal expenditure should be in the neighborhood of $175 billion, or about 30 percent of the projected Gross National Product. In order to achieve this funding, the economy will have to be put on a war footing; economic gyrations of the kind we were experiencing in 1962 will have to be met in a great deal more forceful and effective manner. As in the wars of the past, the huge drain represented by the manufacture and sales of luxury goods will have to be severely curtailed. The expenditures they account for will be channeled to new taxes with which to achieve military parity.

With these and other drastic measures directed at achieving the goals of total victory—the arbitrary allocation of manpower and private facilities, the direction of students into curricula designed to fill professional and technical shortages—the America we now think we are defending would be substantially different from the America of truly overwhelming thermonuclear military capacity. But these are certainly some of the requisites of purely military parity with the Soviet now and China later.

When one faces these demands, it is not hard to see that

it is impossible to adhere to the loose framework set down earlier, that of envisaging a purely *military* set of requirements for nuclear superiority or equality. Vast areas we have hitherto held to be sacrosanct civil and individual activities will be subordinated to military necessity. We are forced, for example, to think of the sheltering of civilians and critical goods, not as simple acts of self-preservation and humanitarian behavior, but as an absolutely vital working part of the war machine, a requirement for believable threat and counterthreat. In this sense, each of us becomes a minuscule unit of the total fighting machine.

The real military dilemma for the democratic power is: How to condition peoples used to thinking of themselves as free to behavior and goals that are the antithesis of freedom? Yet, as things are now going, and hold every promise of continuing to go, the United States will have to rearrange itself in any necessary way to meet the ascending challenges of a rapidly expanding worldwide thermonuclear arsenal. As Oskar Morgenstern recently wrote: "We may look back on 1961 with nostalgia, remembering this as a time when the two great deterrent forces, poised against each other, seemed able to prevent the thermonuclear war. That, we may come to say, was an era of stability."

CHAPTER FIVE

ABOLISHING WAR—
BUT NOT THE SYSTEM

THE PRECEDING CHAPTER HAS DESCRIBED THE POSITION TO
which the war system has brought us and has made what
seems a reasonable extrapolation into the future based upon
presently observable trends. Admittedly, the most thoughtful
extrapolations from history have seldom been justified by the
event. The prediction of inescapable doom that now over-
hangs the world is not really persuasive; yet it is the logical
outcome of everything we now know about international
society. If it is not to be realized, some elements in the
modern predicament must somehow undergo alteration.
The difficulty is to discern what these elements are likely to
be, how they will change, and how change will come about.
   The long search for peace and disarmament may be regarded as a persistent, as it has also been a fruitless, search
for the military, political, or cultural elements in our situa-

tion that if altered would rescue the war system from the dreadful consequences to which it has brought us. The ideas have been many: the simple two-year arms "holiday" initially proposed by the Russians in 1899; the idea of a precisely balanced proportional arms reduction, which would leave every nation relatively as "powerful" as before, but on much lowered levels of cost and terror; the elimination of all "aggressive" weapons while retaining the defensive ones, or (extending this military solution into the political field) the elimination of all "aggressive" militarisms, such as the German was supposed to be, while retaining the full military power of "peace-loving" states. There were the more purely political solutions, such as the early proposals for the extension of arbitral and adjudicatory procedures; the refinement and expansion of international law; the creation of a "collective security" as envisaged in the Covenant of the League of Nations; joint great-power peace enforcement, as envisaged by the unanimity rule in the United Nations Security Council and many other phases of the attempted settlements after 1945; the extinction of all national sovereignty in a "world government." Somehow, by one device or another, the trick could be turned; but it never has been. Despite the fatal flaws that appeared—almost inexplicably, it often seemed—in each of these ideas, many are still prominent and will doubtless have a part in the shaping of the future. But their inadequacy, in sum, is apparent; and today they seem to serve more often as clubs for the rival propagandas than as bases for constructive statesmanship.

The revolutionary appearance of the nuclear arsenals after

1945 made it clearer than ever before that the war problem would have to be resolved; it raised a new possibility that the problem might prove soluble, but quite obviously did not in itself provide a solution. The weapons revolution, like most revolutions, was a consequence of the past, not a design for the future. Given the military-political-technical situation in the mid-nineteenth century, one could almost say that the nuclear weapons, or some similar instruments of military gigantism and mass destruction, were an inevitable end product. But the nuclear physicists had no more prevision than did other revolutionaries (Lenin himself is a good example) of the consequences to which their success might lead. Their excursions into the field of international "power" represent a culmination of the past. The future is a fresh problem.

Until the Soviet achievement, first of the atomic bomb (1949) and then the thermonuclear in the early 1950's, no one really took the war problem too seriously. These great weapons were just more of the same, to which the concepts of nineteenth century or even eighteenth century warfare could be applied with only minor modification. Even today, many students of the subject seem not to realize that it is an *impossible* situation that has been created. They calculate the tens or scores of millions of human beings who might be exterminated in a thermonuclear exchange ("megadeaths" has become a convenient statistical term) as if they were eighteenth century generals calculating the percentages of their little armies that might be lost if they gave battle. It is only in the past four or five years that the real urgency of the weapons problem has impressed itself on American thought. Well into the Eisenhower Administration, two or three rather lowly officials represented the State Department's investment in the disarmament problem; today we have the semiautonomous Arms Control and Disarmament Agency independently staffed as a respected arm of government in this field. For some years now a great deal of hard and earnest thought, official as well as private, has been put into the questions of war and disarmament—more, perhaps, in the United States than in other countries, but by no means confined to the United States. All this labor has not been totally barren—it has doubtless thrown illumination upon some of the "core" difficulties—but has so far produced only faint hopes, at best, for the intrusion of sanity into the modern military political system.

Some of the old, misleading conceptions may have been swept away, though they still thickly encrust the propaganda and policy utterances. Few thoughtful men can seriously believe in the theory of "aggressive" as against "peace-loving" states as an explanation of modern international politics. But "Communist aggression" continues to provide the fuel with which our own arms and foreign policies are stoked; while the notion of the "aggressive" as against the "peace-loving state" is so deeply embedded in the whole Communist ideological and propagandist structure that it seems to be indispensable to Russian statesmanship, even when the Russians know better. After the tragic experience of decades, no one can any longer accept the therapy of an all-around, *paripassu* arms reduction, leaving everyone where they were before. Yet it is still prominent (doubtless for want of anything better) in official American disarmament policy. The analytical work of recent years has tended to discredit the old "matching" theory ("whatever the Soviets have or can do, we must match or exceed"), yet the President can still proclaim the goal of "a nuclear capability second to none," and the claque responds more or less as it did in the days, for example, of Britain's "two keels for one" or Wilson's "incomparably the greatest navy in the world." Not even Khrushchev can really believe that any single, simple plan— whether his own "general and complete disarmament within three years" or something like Clark and Sohn's "world peace through world law" in ten years—has any possible present chance of acceptance. Yet the plans continue to be proposed as essays in serious statesmanship. Instructed by the great weapons, we are a good deal less naïve about the war problem than were our predecessor generations, though the education has admittedly not reached deeply into the popular consciousness. If it seems to have reached even less deeply into the Russian consciousness, that is something that cannot be helped. We have to fashion our world out of the elements that exist within it. We cannot hope to command Russian policy, though we can perhaps influence it, and we cannot rationally design a world in which the Soviet Union and China do not exist. All we can do is to hope that the best of the Russians and Chinese are beginning to see the world society as our studies are suggesting that it exists in fact, and to adopt those lines of policy and of propaganda that will facilitate the processes of reason in the other powers. For the rest, we are forced to do the best with the world problem for ourselves that we can.

In this endeavor, several lines of thought have emerged out of the work of the past few years. None seems very hopeful. They are overlapping; their principal spokesmen do not always appear to accept the consequences of their own positions; one can classify them only roughly, but an attempt at classification seems useful. They include:

a) The "fight it out" approach. Here the hope, and no doubt the expectation as well, is that there will be no thermonuclear war. But the argument is that the best way of reducing the probability of such a war, without inacceptable "surrender," is by naked reliance on military "power." This, however, involves the paradox that to reduce the probability of the war, the nation must act on the assumption that it is highly probable and could be sustained and survived. All practicable preparations both to fight and to survive it— from a "counterforce" weapons system to fallout shelters— must be taken. This, it is hardly necessary to point out, provides no resolution whatever for the war dilemma. It simply accepts the war system as it now stands; it offers no hope of canceling or even slowing the arms race; it tends to maximize every danger of war by miscalculation or accident, and seems to many to make the ultimate thermonuclear catastrophe inevitable.

b) The approach through "deterrence." The hope here is that the now unmanageable weapons systems can be balanced so nicely as to "deter" resort to them by any state. But again one finds oneself involved in paradox. Several years ago

Albert Wohlstetter of RAND Corporation pointed to the great technical difficulties in the way of establishing a really stable "balance of terror." [1] The problem, however, is much more than technical. It raises an issue few exponents of "deterrence" have ever faced fairly. Is the object of "deterrence" to *prevent* thermonuclear war absolutely, or only to render resort to it more difficult, inconvenient, and therefore less probable? If the latter is the case, the theoreticians of deterrence do not seem to differ greatly from the "fight it out" school, and their concrete proposals run closely parallel. If the object of deterrence on the other hand, is absolutely to prevent a thermonuclear war, one runs again into trouble. Concrete proposals by those who have tried seriously to follow this approach to its logical conclusion soon end in sheer fantasy. The attempt to abolish thermonuclear war by strictly military means leads to such results as the "Doomsday Machine," invented and described (but never recommended) by Herman Kahn. This is a system that will absolutely deter resort to war by anyone, through ensuring the total and automatic destruction of humanity if any state goes to war.

Another equally logical consequence of military deterrence as an absolute preventive are the "mined cities" that Leo Szilard's dolphins have proposed. [2] In this scheme a hydrogen bomb is securely buried under every important American and Russian city, each bomb being under the control of a crew drawn from the other nation. If a city on either side is

[1] RAND Corporation Report P–1472, November, 1958.
[2] *Bulletin of Atomic Scientists*, December, 1961, p. 407.

obliterated by nuclear attack, the corresponding city on the other side will be obliterated by the crew stationed there for the purpose; in this event, no cities will be obliterated, and there will be no thermonuclear war. The logic of this is impressive. It does no more than carry the hostage principle, on which all present theories of deterrence rest, to its rational conclusion. It would accomplish everything that the gigantic Soviet and American deterrent forces are now accomplishing in fact, and would do it at vastly less cost and with much greater certainty. Yet such a scheme is obviously fantastic and impossible. If it is at the same time a logical extrapolation from deterrence theory, it would seem simply to expose the fantasy hidden within the theory. Earlier, Szilard had proposed a less complicated scheme whereby the United States and the USSR draw up a "menu" of equivalent cities and punish each other on a one-to-one basis when sufficiently provoked. The core of the idea was that the people would be removed well in advance of the calculated nuclear exchange, reducing the attrition to highly prized real estate. This eminently practical reduction of the total-war concept is widely viewed as pure satire.

In itself, military deterrence is either a device for postponing a thermonuclear exchange—at the cost of making it more certainly catastrophic when it arrives; or it is a device for rendering such an exchange *impossible,* which in the absence of a profound change in attitude toward the whole system of war itself, can be done only through fantastically dangerous measures that no government or people would today dream of accepting.

c) The approach through graduated or "controlled dis-armament." This is the line along which United Nations and other disarmament efforts have been working for years, without any noticeable result. One may suspect that the basic reason for this ill-success is, as with "deterrence," the fact that the disarmers have never clearly known what results they expected to achieve by the reduction of armaments. Everyone agrees that things would be more comfortable if there were fewer dangerous weapons lying about the world, but not many have addressed themselves to the difficult ques-tion of what a world with fewer weapons available in it would really be like. Progress along this line has, in any event, been minimal. The Russians and the West have at times come rather close to what seemed to be agreement on large plans for mutual, graduated, and inspected disarma-ment; Philip Noel-Baker has gone so far as to say that in 1954 agreement was virtually complete and was destroyed only by Western reversal. But this is illusion. There has never been any real agreement; and it is significant that the break-down point has usually come, whether in general disarma-ment or in the test-ban and similar peripheral issues, over the question of "inspection."

Americans have been inclined to ascribe the inspection difficulties variously to an inbred Russian love of secrecy for its own sake; to a supposed Russian strategic doctrine emphasizing secrecy as a strategic weapon; to the hesitations of the regime over opening their own masses to Western in-filtration and knowledge of Western conditions. Such factors are no doubt present. But to stress them is to overlook the fundamental fact that inspection is power. The Russians may say that Western demands to control disarmament agreements are merely "espionage" devices, inadmissible until the West has totally and convincingly resigned any idea or possibility of waging war on Russia. The West may react to such a position with righteous indignation. It is fully willing to be inspected by Russians; why cannot the Soviet Union reciprocate—unless it is actually scheming to bind the West in disarmament procedures that it intends to and will itself evade? The Soviet Union has, of course, offered to reciprocate—but only under the proviso that it retains a veto power over the inspecting authority, as it would under its "troika" plan for a tripartite administration of disarmament. The first Western response to the "troika" idea was that it was totally inadmissible—simply another device through which the Russians would retain their freedom to evade any armament agreement into which they might entrap the West. But there have been at least some second thoughts in the West. If "troika" is totally unacceptable, what can the West offer in its place?

If one is seriously contemplating a disarming world, one must ask seriously how it is to be administered. The West will certainly not permit it to be administered by the Communist states; and the Communist states will no less certainly prevent its administration by the Western states. The Russians have proposed a three-headed administration by Communist, Western, and "neutralist" powers. The proposal has its appeal. The West, however, has many perfectly sound reasons for rejecting this solution to the dilemma. The difficulty is that it has no solution of its own and does not always seem to realize that a dilemma exists.

The issue over "inspection" is nothing new. It is merely a transference into a particular area of concern of the basic power issue that appears to be inescapable, in whatever terms it is phrased or presented, so long as war and military threat remain the only ultimate bases of international relations. In any presently imaginable disarmament agreement, the power of inspection will be the power of control. If a genuinely international or supranational authority existed, accepted as such alike by Communist, Western, and neutralist states, it would be simple to confide to it the inspection and control of disarmament agreements. The United Nations is obviously not such an authority and cannot be made into one. To what authority can inspection be given, without upsetting the present balances of military power?

The Soviet answer from the beginning has been the same —a joint great-power organization operating under the unanimity rule. Experience would seem to show that it is not a very good or useful answer in existing contexts. Yet the West really has no other; it is the answer to which the West itself has always clung, and for which it has been able to offer no better alternative.

The issue is always over power. In the particular question of "inspected disarmament," it is the same issue, and just as insusceptible to resolution by military or mechanical means as it is in other contexts. Many ingenious ideas have been advanced for setting up adequately effective systems for inspecting and ensuring compliance with disarmament agreements. There are the methods for detecting atomic explosion by physical means (such as manned or unmanned seismological detectors); the "spot-check" methods; the "area inspection" methods; the psychological methods (such as offering massive rewards for any citizen who will betray his own country's violation of the agreement); and many more. All, it is believed, proceed from a fundamentally mistaken assumption; and it may be predicted with some confidence that no "iron-clad" or "completely effective" inspection and control system of this kind will ever be established. To say, as most Western statesmen do, that disarmament depends upon absolute guarantees as to compliance is to say that no disarmament is as yet possible. Disarmament will begin to get under way only when it is generally seen to be unavoidable; and at that point no one will care very much about whether all the provisions are complied with or not. This point will be further elaborated later; for the moment it is enough to say that the arms will begin to disappear only when they are seen to be *useless* as well as highly dangerous; and if they are useless, whether disarmament provisions are respected or not will make little difference. Until that time, "controlled disarmament" is as feeble an approach to the war problem as the others that have been considered.

d) The approach through "arms control." Russian writers, and possibly some Western pacifists, are inclined to regard "arms control" as no more than a red herring drawn by imperialists and warmongers across the path of Khrushchev's "general and complete disarmament." They may be right to the extent that it represents a recoil from the appalling problems of peace and demilitarization (problems to which the Russians have brought no more helpful solutions than anyone else), but its backgrounds are really more respectable than this would suggest. It represents an earnest attempt to escape the very real dilemmas posed by the other military approaches to the war problem. It was not mere cynicism that led to the change in the designation of the new agency to make it the *"Arms Control* and Disarmament Agency." The arms controllers are no doubt as divided among themselves as are other laborers in this field, but what distinguishes them from the advocates of "disarmament" is their insistence that the primary problem is not necessarily the reduction of armaments but their stabilization. Initially, at least, a stabilized "balance of terror"—whatever the levels of cost or terror—is preferable to an unstable military balance on much lower levels.

Arms control is really "deterrence" in a more sophisticated form. Probably most thoughtful arms controllers would admit that it is at best a stopgap solution—something to tide us over the next few perilous years, but in no sense a design for a permanent international order. Arms control argues in general for stable deterrence for the nuclear weapons (for invulnerable "second-strike" forces with no "first-strike" or counterforce capability) plus "limited war" forces to deal on the lowest practicable level of violence with such issues as may arise under a continuance of the war system itself. As a design for organizing a viable and enduring world politics, the objections to this are many; but as a temporary and transitional expedient, arms control is entitled to respect. If arms control can keep the peace until the world is ready to abolish the war system altogether, it will have served its purpose; if it cannot, humanity's game is lost anyway, and the arms controllers will be less responsible than others for the ultimate disaster. In the existing international context, arms control appears to be a useful approach to the problem, but except as a stopgap its potentialities are limited and it offers no foundation on which to build a viable world order.

e) The approach through "unilateral disarmament." Because it attempts to bring basic political and psychological factors into the equation, this is more interesting than the purely military approaches, and actually has a greater theoretical validity than is usually recognized. Unfortunately, the hopes of any practical advance that it holds out seem slim indeed. The minimal approach, as developed by Charles Osgood and others, suggests only that it is possible for the United States independently to take certain small steps toward disarmament, of a kind that will not materially impair its real military security but might invite the Soviet Union to imitation. If this follows, further unilateral steps might be taken, with hope of further imitation, and so on to a general reduction in the pressure of the weaponry. Aside, however, from the technical difficulties of selecting the initial steps and assuring ourselves that the Russians are really following suit, the process is bound soon to reach the point at which further divestment does trench upon the military power positions of the nations. It will then come to an abrupt halt. Unless one can disarm beyond the point at which divestment *will* affect the national "security," one can hardly travel far down this road.

The approach is valuable, however, in emphasizing the fact that we should always try to put the least, rather than the greatest, stress upon the value of the weapons. Today, it is enough to tag almost any measure as a "military necessity," or requisite for us to "stay ahead of the Russians," for billions to pour out in its support, no matter how fantastic it may be or how remote from any probable military utility. A rather bolder "unilateral" approach argues that in the process we have got so far ahead of the Russians already that we could simply suspend the arms race on our side regardless of whether the Russians followed suit or not. (According to Gerard Piel we already "outgun" the Soviet Union with our nuclear striking force by five to one.) Indeed, a really earnest pursuit of "arms control" and stabilization might come to a similar conclusion; it would certainly have to revalue the real military uses of the existing weapons systems. A mere suspension, unilaterally, of the arms race would certainly be of the utmost help, but even if it could be made politically practicable it would still be only a temporary answer to the war problem.

The maximum form of "unilateralism," exemplified by Bertrand Russell or Stephen King-Hall in Britain and Mulford Sibley in America, declares flatly that the weapons are of no use to anyone anyway and that the West might better sink its whole panoply in the ocean tomorrow, leaving the Russians to cling to their arsenals if they wanted to. Curiously enough, this looks as though it really might work.

Assuming a Soviet Union armed to the teeth with nuclear weapons and confronting a Western and neutralist world that had divested itself of such "power," what could the Soviet Union actually do with its armament? It could, of course, make demands and threats on pain of nuclear extermination. But if the demands were simply rejected, could the power of extermination help them at all? Would their military power not in fact be reduced to the position of the French military power in Europe after 1918, which in the absence of a German army had no target against which to direct its efforts and in the result lost all control over events in Central Europe? Such questions are suggestive, and hint at the erosion of all military power, which it is here argued must sooner or later occur. Unilateral disarmament in this form offers the most logical avenue to the solution of the world problem; but it is patently impossible without massive transformation in the political and cultural frameworks surrounding the war system, of a kind which are out of the question today.

f) The primarily political approaches. With each of the military approaches to the war problem apparently leading to a complete dead end, one is forced to ask whether political devices may not extricate them. Of these, many have been proposed. They would seem to fall into two general catagories: specific proposals for achieving a *détente* in existing international issues, and general proposals for establishing some form of world order capable of dealing with any threat of war that may arise or any specific issues that may originate anywhere now or later. Under the first head there

are the many proposals for dealing with the Formosa problem or, particularly, the problem of Berlin and the two
Germanies. Once such current issues have been rationally
"negotiated," the great military powers can move on with
confidence to the problem of divesting themselves of their
weaponry. In the second category there fall the many plans—
from the simple "strengthening of the United Nations" to
the most elaborate proposals for world federalism—designed
to replace the existing international "anarchy" with an effective but nonmilitary rule of law.

Both these forms of approach, it must be noted, at least
tacitly assume the continued existence of the war system as
the fundamental regulator of international affairs, which is
perhaps the reason why they have made so little progress.
The various specific plans for Central Europe, for example,
would seek to remove what now seems a most likely "cause"
for war between the great powers, but would leave the great
armaments and great military powers unaffected. The difficulty here is that the real "cause" of war is not the Germanies; it is the armaments and military powers. It is not
difficult to devise a rational and reasonably just solution
for the problems of the Germans, or even of the Germans
vis-à-vis the rest of Europe. What has proved impossible
so far is to devise a solution of the German problem that
will satisfy the power issues between the Soviet Union, the
United States and the West. The West cannot abandon
Adenauer because if it did its power position in Europe
would be destroyed; the Russians cannot abandon Ulbricht
(who is probably even more a pain to them than Adenauer

to his Western supporters) for precisely the same reason. So long as the basic war system endures, it is improbable that any "political" solution for the dilemmas it raises can permanently succeed.

The second category of political solutions of course encounters the same difficulty, but in exaggerated form. If it is difficult to arrive at agreement over current specific problems, it is surely virtually impossible to arrive at agreement over any system that will profess to solve not only current but also any future problems under generalized legal procedures. If one cannot find a workable answer to the Germanies in 1962, how can one hope to design a structure that will not only resolve this problem but also resolve all others of a similar character throughout the foreseeable future? Once more one is compelled to say that there is no *present* hope. All the proposed solutions, military and political, will no doubt play their part in the developing future (if one may assume that we have a future), but none in itself is sufficient or persuasive. Something else must somehow be introduced into the equation. War can be controlled neither by military nor by political means. The only real answer is that the war system must itself be abolished, if it is not to abolish us.

It is interesting (though not, one fears, too hopeful) that this is the answer at which the world's two greatest military powers have officially arrived. Both are formally committed to the abolition of the war system itself, through the "general and complete" demilitarization of the world. In his address of September, 1961, Kennedy accepted the phrase advanced by Khrushchev two or three years before. The joint statement of principles, submitted by the United States and the Soviet Union to the United Nations on September 20, 1961, at least appears to go a long way:

The goal of negotiations is to ensure that disarmament is general and complete and war is no longer an instrument for settling international problems, [that] . . . . such disarmament is accompanied by reliable procedures for the peaceful settlement of international disputes . . . that states will have at their disposal only those non-nuclear armaments . . . as are agreed to be necessary to maintain internal order . . . and that states shall support and provide manpower for a UN peace force.

[Armed forces, bases, war production, and so on to be] disbanded and discontinued . . . by stages . . . within specified time limits . . .

All measures . . . should be balanced so that at no stage . . . could any state or group of states gain military advantage and that security is assured equally for all.

[There should be] such strict and effective international control as would provide firm assurance that all parties are honoring their obligations. . . .

Progress in disarmament should be accompanied by institutions for maintaining peace and the settlement of international disputes by peaceful means.

Here is agreement between the world's two most powerful military states upon the overall objective—the demilitarization of the world society—and upon what must at first glance seem a very reasonable set of principles by which to attain it. It certainly brings all the very best butter (churned over some sixty years of effort) to the repair of the watch—

from the resignation of war as "an instrument of policy," which was in the Kellogg Pact in the mid-1920's, to "strict international control" of disarmament undertakings, which is the current preoccupation. Yet there is probably no serious student of the matter who believes for a moment that the principles can be applied or the announced objective can be brought one step nearer. The Soviet Union and the United States both stand committed to the demilitarization of the world. There seems to be no other possible exit from the modern dilemma. But neither the Soviet Union nor the United States has offered any practical guidance as to how this essential goal can practically be attained.

CHAPTER SIX

A POSSIBLE
FUTURE

"THE GOAL," ACCORDING TO THE AGREED AMERICAN AND Soviet statement of principles, is to "ensure that disarmament is general and complete and war is no longer an instrument for settling international problems." Both parties may profoundly distrust the motives of the other in proclaiming this goal, but the fact remains that there is no other practicable or possible resolution of the modern dilemma. With all the various military and military-political solutions doomed almost demonstrably to failure in the future (as all have consistently failed so far), one is forced to the only remaining alternative—a demilitarized world, necessitating the abolition of the war system and the end of organized international war.

It is intellectually easier and more comfortable to continue to play with ideas of an indefinite stabilization of the war system, of a reduction in its levels of terror and destructiveness; but no long-term policy can be constructed out of these concepts, while unless and until the demilitarization of the global system is consciously and earnestly accepted as the ultimate goal, it is unlikely that much interim progress can be made with them. The choice, which has been narrowing over the past century, has narrowed sharply with the nuclear revolution; until we can now say with confidence that it is a choice between the ultimate demilitarization or the ultimate destruction of our civilization. The Soviet-American statement of principles means that on this the two powers are agreed; and perhaps this is a good deal. Unfortunately, it is obvious that they are agreed on almost nothing else.

The very way in which the statement is phrased—"to ensure that disarmament is general and complete and war is no longer an instrument for settling international problems"—conceals a critical difference in approach. This is like saying: "Our goal is to ensure that eggs are eliminated and that chickens are no longer to be instrumental in meeting international food problems." Which comes first? If chickens are dispensed with, there will be no difficulty about eliminating the eggs; if the eggs are eliminated, there will be no difficulty about dispensing with chickens as a food resource. The Russian position is that if all agree to abolish the chickens (war), all problems as to the armament eggs—inspection, compliance, control, international police, and so on—become easily manageable. The Western position is that if you agree gradually to abolish the eggs (armaments), the chickens of war that hatch from them will gradually disappear in the process, and the war problem will become manageable.

Of the two views, the Russian is, superficially, much the more logical. There can really be little doubt that it is the great weapons systems themselves—with all the fears and ambitions that they engender—that are the major "causes" of war between modern, highly integrated states. The only way to get rid of war is to get rid of it—entirely—and once this has been done, actually or prospectively, the new sociopolitical situation that must result will be self-sustaining and self-perpetuating. In an arresting paper, David F. Cavers has argued that once the process of general disarmament to police-force level had been started, it would set up a kind of political chain reaction, each step hastening and reinforcing the next, in which the presently insuperable problems of inspection and compliance would dissolve of themselves. Leo Szilard's amusing and satiric fantasies of the future usually show a much harder grasp of the realities than can be found in the stodgier and more "realistic" discussions of disarmament experts. Szilard's imaginary disarmament conferences of 1987–1988 have little difficulty with problems of inspection and compliance under conditions of virtually complete disarmament; the hard problem, in his imaginary future as it is today, is in getting the movement toward total disarmament started.

The Russians would abolish war in order to make disarmament possible; the West would start a process of gradual reduction of armaments in order to make the abolition of war

possible, meanwhile clinging at every step to all the supposed
safeties and securities of the war system, until finally assured
that war is no longer necessary to it. That this is bound to be
self-defeating it should hardly be necessary to argue, though
the point is beautifully illustrated by the long wrangle over a
ban on nuclear testing. As originally conceived, the test ban
had an admirable directness and simplicity. Since air bursts
of nuclear weapons are in at least some degree dangerous to
all humanity, and since they are quite readily detectable, an
agreement to discontinue them would be simple and self-
enforcing. With both the American and the Soviet governments favorable to the idea, one might suppose than an agreement could have been written in an afternoon. Years
afterward, there is still (at the end of 1962) no agreement.

To raise the idea was to focus attention upon the possible
military advantages of further testing. Then it appeared that
even if air bursts were banned, undetectable underground
(and possibly outer-space) tests might still be conducted. The
Russian view was that there should be a general undertaking
to discontinue all tests, detectable or undetectable. The American view was that the United States could not bind itself to
discontinue all forms of testing unless it had assurance that
the Russians were not violating their corresponding undertaking by conducting undiscoverable underground tests.
Matters thus proceeded until it was found that a system for
certainly monitoring small underground tests would be far
more difficult and expensive to establish than had at first been
supposed. By this time, the question of security against pos-

sible violation by the other side had been raised beyond all proportion to the practical military-technical issues involved.

American policy was, in effect, confronted with a choice. It could have a Soviet undertaking to halt any further testing of any kind, in return for a similar undertaking by the United States. This would put an effective, self-enforcing, end to the dangerous air bursts; it would engage the Soviet Union not to conduct underground bursts, but would give no positive assurance that the Soviet Union would honor its engagement. Or the United States could reject the Soviet offer, in the hope of forcing the USSR into accepting a hugely expensive and politically dangerous inspection system that would guarantee USSR performance of the undertaking not to conduct underground experiments. Presumably, this choice must have been weighed by American policy-makers, in the AEC or the National Security Council or elsewhere. If so, no intelligible account of the argument has ever reached the general public. On what grounds, military, political, or technical, it was determined that the very great advantages of a joint agreement to conduct no further testing at all were outweighed by the military advantages the Russians might gain by conducting clandestine underground tests was never explained. Yet such was the determination.

A fantastic interlude ensued in which the Americans sought to force the Russians to accept their completely controlled test ban by threatening to resume testing if the Russians did not accept. The Russians similarly sought to put pressure on the Americans to accept their uncontrolled test ban. This was certainly fatuous on the American side, since the last thing the Americans wanted was a resumption of any sort of testing. Russian motivation is less clear. Whether, if the Americans had accepted the uncontrolled ban (which would have effectively ended air testing) the Russians would have stood by it, or whether, for military reasons, they were anxious to resume air testing and were simply maneuvering the Americans into a position in which the Americans could not prevent a resumption of such tests, we do not know. The result, at any rate, was the massive series of Russian air bursts in the fall of 1961. These were of far greater importance to weapons development than concealable low-yield bursts underground, they could have been prevented by our agreement to a general ban; and they were soon being anxiously scrutinized by our technical experts to find whether they had given Russian weaponry an important "lead" over our own. Whether they did or not, the Americans had been maneuvered or had maneuvered themselves, into a position that made the usual riposte (resuming air bursts on our own part) difficult and embarrassing.

The public argument for resumption of American testing rested on the familiar "arms race" arguments, those which contended that the Russians had used the informal moratorium period for intense preparation of tests that might lead to an overwhelming "breakthrough" that would hopelessly shatter the deterrent balance. There was considerable technical and emotional force to these contentions. Men such as Hans Bethe appear to have been sufficiently shaken by the possible implications of the Russian series to have made dramatic shifts in their previously held positions against

American test resumption. Fortified by outside opinions such as these, influential technical groups within the Department of Defense and the Atomic Energy Commission joined with a majority of the members of the Joint Congressional Committee on Atomic Energy in urging the President to resume atmospheric testing. He proved unable to resist these persuasions for long, and entered the Geneva disarmament negotiations in March with a position that made their breakdown virtually inevitable. American tests were resumed in May.

By attempting in this instance to cling to the supposed protections of the war system while endeavoring to reduce its impact, the United States made the worst of both worlds. A broader approach to the test-ban problem, capable of taking political and psychological as well as crassly military considerations into account, might have led to happier results. This is commonly said to have been impossible because the United States cannot "trust" the Russians. But this is a mistaken way of looking at the matter. No nation, of course, ever can or does trust another beyond the limits to which mutual self-interest extends; and confidence cannot be pushed beyond those limits by even the most perfect systems for proving the other side to be cheating. The point is not that the United States should have put greater "trust" in the USSR, but that it should have made a shrewder analysis of the factors of self-interest involved on both sides. This would, it is believed, have indicated that it was improbable that the Russians would violate a general test ban and that even if they succeeded in doing so without detection the military gains to them would not really have been of major importance, and certainly far less than the military and political gains for the United States through securing the general ban on all further testing. But the test-ban negotiations, by the very fact that they focused all attention on the weapons systems themselves, to the exclusion of all the human and political factors surrounding them, rendered this sort of analysis virtually impossible. At the end of 1962 there was evidence of some second thoughts on both sides, suggesting that such analysis might not be so impossible after all. But the episode remains as one more of many illustrations of the truth that one cannot reduce or suppress weapons systems by negotiatory processes that must attach maximum, rather than minimum, political and cultural values to the military power of the weapons one is trying to suppress.

The Russians are quite right in their argument that the only way to disarm is to abolish war. Certainly, a gradual disarmament program, which clings tenaciously to all the supposed values of the war system as it proceeds, is most unlikely to proceed at all. The obvious defect in the Russians' position is, however, that it gives no indication of how they propose to abolish war, of what contributions they propose to make to this consummation, or of how they anticipate that the resultant demilitarized world will operate. Disarmament proposals predicated, in effect, upon the prior abolition of the war system, and which can proceed only as there is general agreement that the war system be laid aside, are equally unlikely to proceed at all unless they can give some hint as to how this agreement might be brought about. It is all very well for Khrushchev and Kennedy to adopt a common goal of general and complete disarmament and the elimination of war as an instrument of national policy. But so long as neither statesman can really face the implications of his own position, the goal will almost certainly remain, in the practical contexts of international affairs, of only propagandist significance.

If it is true that the modern choice is between demilitarization and destruction, something more than all this is desperately needed. It is here argued that two things, specifically, are needed. The first is a reasonably clear and persuasive picture of how a demilitarized world could be expected to operate—what institutional arrangements it would require, how these institutions would function, what fundamental cultural changes it would demand or would itself produce, what securities it would guarantee and what sacrifices it would exact. And—most significant of all—how it would resolve the power issues that are inherent in human life, national or international, which in the past have normally been confided to the arbitrament of organized war, and for which a demilitarized world would have to find some other means of resolution.

The second thing that is needed is some idea of how the process of general demilitarization can in fact be initiated. It will be argued here that (as has already been suggested) the process once started will prove self-sustaining and that the end result—a demilitarized world—should be highly stable. But to get the process under way would seem to call for profound changes in present-day political and cultural concepts.

How far these changes must extend, and what the possibilities are that they may begin to be of effect before we are overtaken by thermonuclear extermination, are questions demanding careful attention now. Indeed, the two requirements—a clear and persuasive picture of how the demilitarized world would operate, and a clear concept of how such a world might in fact be generated—are so closely interrelated that there may be a certain artificiality in attempting to separate them. For the purposes of the present discussion, however, this division appears to assist in clarifying the argument, and it is here adopted.

The design of a demilitarized world is, it is believed, a good deal less difficult, and much less Utopian, than is usually assumed. For one thing, we already have large working models of effectively demilitarized international societies, providing us with concrete experimental material in this area, the significance of which seems often overlooked. It is true that none of these models successfully bridges the chasm between the Communist and the non-Communist worlds, but they do provide important data upon the actual behavior of the highly integrated modern sovereign nation-state under conditions of effective demilitarization. And they are data that dispute many of the more generalized fears as to the consequences of a global demilitarization as well as some of the more elaborate notions as to what would be required to effect and sustain a global demilitarization.

The most useful and important of these working models is the North Atlantic Treaty Organization. There can be little doubt that the fourteen sovereign states who are members of NATO (together with some others, such as Sweden, Switzerland, Ireland, Spain) are effectively demilitarized as regards each other. These are the states that have waged among themselves (at times, to be sure, with outside assistance) almost all the important wars in modern history. Today, a war ranging any of them against one or others in the group seems as near to an impossibility as anything in the future can be. For present purposes it is unnecessary to ask how this situation has arisen; it is enough to ask how the relations of this community of mutually demilitarized sovereign states are in fact conducted, how the "disputes" that continue to arise between them are settled, what institutional devices have or have not seemed prerequisite to the maintenance of peace and order among them.

If one examines the North Atlantic Alliance and its associated states from this point of view, a number of suggestive conclusions emerge. There can be little doubt in the first place that they are mutually demilitarized. Most of them maintain large military establishments, but these establishments are not designed or organized to fight each other. For many reasons it would be technically difficult for them to do so—because large portions of their forces are earmarked for the NATO unified command, because of their common weapons systems and logistic bases, because of the complications surrounding the joint control of the tactical nuclear weapons. These technical disabilities are immensely compounded by the overweening political and economic control of the United States, upon which the whole military system depends. Thus another war like those of 1914 and 1939, involving France, Germany, Britain, Italy, and the United States, has been rendered as impossible as another war like that of 1861 involving the several states of the American Union.

This effective demilitarization has been accompanied, whether as cause or effect, by other suggestive developments. They have brought profound changes in the political and cultural attitudes of Western Europeans. Frenchmen and Germans today do not regard each other with anything like the prejudices that obtained on both sides of the border in 1914 and in 1939. There continue to be differences and disputes, some of a major character, among the members of the North Atlantic system, but no one imagines that they could be usefully resolved by resort to organized war. There are serious practical issues, such as those surrounding the question of British association with the European Common Market and American trade and tariff policies in respect to it, but no one has suggested that war would be a usable instrument of policy in such issues; and they are being gradually worked out by negotiatory processes that can proceed, fundamentally, because the negotiators do not have war as a possible alternative to adjustment. There are even issues of abstract "power" within the alliance—issues of the kind that has always seemed unsusceptible to resolution except by the trial at arms—which no one expects to eventuate in war. There are European resentments against the abstract "power" of the United States; there are American resentments against De Gaulle's attempt to acquire the nuclear symbols of "power"—which cannot for a long time, if ever, be turned into an operable power on the actual world stage. Such contests over "power" and "glory" within the alliance may be expected to continue, but no one thinks that battle either must or can be the "payoff." Within the alliance, the power balances will shift, but it will not again take a bloody inter-NATO war to record the change.

Another cliché that experience calls in question is that which assumes that a prerequisite to a demilitarized world is a developed system of global law, capable of resolving all international "disputes" by juridical means backed by coercive powers of enforcement. Such institutions, not merely of international but of supranational juridical authority, appear to be developing within the North Atlantic complex—the Court of Justice of the European Coal and Steel Community is an example—but they are developing as a consequence rather than as a cause of demilitarization. They enjoy supranational authority in those areas where it is clearly in the interests of the participating states to accord it; but they have no supranational coercive or police powers. When the NATO Treaty was ratified in 1949, it made no provision for a supranational government, no provision for an inter-NATO judiciary to "settle disputes," and no provision for an inter-NATO police force with coercive powers. Even the unified NATO military command was not developed until later, when the developing power relations in the Western world made both the necessity for and the fact of effective intra-Western demilitarization apparent. Such institutional changes and developments as were requisite to take account of this fact have tended to appear as they are needed. When global power relations make a global demilitarization both possible and unavoidable, the institutional modifications will follow in due course.

A similar model of a demilitarized international system appears to be provided by the Western Hemisphere. There has not been an international war between or among any of the twenty-two sovereign states within the Hemisphere for the past thirty years or so. While all but one (Costa Rica) maintain formal military establishments, most of them actually amount to little more than the national police forces envisaged by all proposals for general disarmament. They have been used only as such police forces would be; they do not plan or prepare war against other members of the group and have not been employed by their governments to back up military threats against other states. The defection of Cuba to the Communist camp and its extensive armament with Communist weapons may alter this situation, but it does not seem to have done so as yet. So far Castro has in fact confined his aggressive and expansionist tendencies to the nonmilitary methods of propaganda and subversion. Until the discovery of the Soviet missiles and bombers in Cuba, it was these methods, rather than the Castro armaments, that alarmed other members of the group. Too little is known about the reasons for the Soviet export and subsequent withdrawal of the weapons to estimate the ultimate significance of this episode. But so far it has led to no move toward re-armament on the part of the other American states. Most of them are struggling with severe social and economic problems; but to none has it occurred that they could be resolved by resort to organized war. Like others among the smaller nations, they may even see that the vast debilitation of the giant states by the war system only denies to them the resources that could and should go into their own social and economic rehabilitation.

All this has come about without even as rudimentary a structure of international governance as is provided in the NATO system. Differences and disputes of course arise among the members of the group, but they are not susceptible to resolution by war—as the United States discovered when confronted with the Castro problem. In fact, wars do not really proceed from "disputes"; they proceed from underlying power issues that specific disputes do no more than catalyze. The power relations in the Western Hemisphere are not such, even after the intrusion of the struggle between the Communists and the non-Communists, as to make organized war a practicable instrument of policy. Even in the weapons crisis the United States, while using military force to police the situation, was very careful to avoid threatening war in order to secure the removal of the missiles.

These situations, of course, present models only; and it may be argued that they are not models applicable to the full-scale global structure. It may be said that it is only the overriding power struggle between the Communists and non-Communists that has made possible the development of the power structures within NATO or the Western Hemisphere that have permitted these examples of international demilitarization. It does, indeed, seem obvious that the processes of global demilitarization—of general and complete disarmament—cannot be initiated without a *détente* in the struggle between Communists and non-Communists, and our models do not throw much light—they may throw some —on how this can be brought about. For the moment, however, this is another question. The immediate concern is with the design of a world demilitarized, not with the more difficult problem of its construction.

Since demilitarization is apparently impossible without it, one is justified in beginning by assuming the existence of a *détente* among the four or five great centers of military power—the United States, the Soviet Union, Western Europe, Great Britain (or Britain with Western Europe), and China —extending at least as far as that which exists today among the NATO powers or those of the Western Hemisphere. It would have to include a final liquidation of the Second World War (much as the former Western Allies have liquidated their differences with Germany, Italy, and Austria) and the effective resignation of any serious irredentist or territorial claims by one power against another. It would have to include an operative understanding among all (like that which exists within the North Atlantic grouping) that whatever differences might arise among them could not be settled by resort to organized war and would have to be resolved by other means. It would have to include a realization on the part of each of the great power centers that the others were permanent parts of the landscape of the age; that it was hopeless to dream of resolving conflicts between them by the destruction of one or another. These are the minimum conditions for a demilitarized world. But they are not Utopian. Urged on by the nuclear terrors, we are not impossibly far from them even today. Since 1945 the great powers have at least been acting as if such a *détente* already existed, even when they have not talked as though it did.

It is assumed, therefore, that the demilitarized world begins with an effective, even if more or less tacit, agreement of this kind among the four or five major power centers. Each has the size, in land area and population, and the industrial and economic development to make it a viable system of human organization in itself—largely self-contained, and if not fully "autarchic" at least with no unappeasable demands upon the peoples, territories, and resources of the others that would seem to it a rational cause of war.[1] Each will be dis-

[1] The assumption here is that China will develop along much the same lines as the Soviet Union has done. She has not done so as yet, and the combination, in the Chinese case, of an enormous and growing population with a backwardness of industrial development which may fail to overtake it admittedly raises a question as to the assumption. Will not "population pressure" drive the Chinese into aggressive expansion into the less populated areas of Siberia or Australasia? To many, this question is enough to dispose at once of any question of a warless world. I do not think the answer is so simple. The relation of "population pressure" to war may be obvious in the case of the ancient migratory tribes; its relation to the modern wars of the modern highly integrated states is anything but obvious. Though Hitler's demands for *Lebensraum* were among his most powerful propaganda weapons, few would seriously attribute the Second World War to the pressure of German population; nor, conversely, argue that it was the population pressure on the Soviet Government that dictated its resistance, its repulse of the Germans, or the extensions of its political power in 1944 and 1945. The border warfare between China and India cannot, certainly, be attributed to population pressures. It is strategic, not demographic. There is little reason to suppose that Chinese, any more than Indian, leaders will conclude that a disparity between population and resources can be cured by war, when many more efficient means are available.

armed to police-force level. It is believed that there has been no very serious study of just what "police-force level" means. But it must mean at least that the war offices, general staffs, military mobilization and reserve systems will have been dismantled; that all heavy weapons systems, nuclear and nonnuclear, will have been discarded and war industries converted to nonmilitary uses. The great powers will thus be reduced substantially to the present position of the great majority of sovereign states today, few of which have significant war industries of their own and not many of which maintain heavy weapons in important numbers even when they are available from foreign suppliers. The military establishments of the smaller powers are for the most part not really capable of foreign war; generally speaking, their equipment and organization give them little more than the capability of maintaining internal order and controlling their frontiers against border raids or in matters of customs and immigration. The great-power police forces in a demilitarized world will have to be capable of this much. For the purpose they will doubtless require more than nightsticks and pistols; but even if their equipment includes such things as light tanks, machine guns, or patrol airplanes, their organizational and command systems will not be conducive to their use for aggression upon their neighbors. Such national police forces, moreover, having laid aside their intercontinental rockets, bomber fleets, naval carrier forces and submarine fleets, can have effect only upon their immediate neighbors. In general, the five giant power centers are not contiguous.

There is a common border between the Soviet Union and China, but most will probably feel that this is already as completely demilitarized, by political and power factors, as the border between the United States and Canada. The Communist and the Western systems meet in Central Europe, but only in a complex of satellite states. This border is dangerous and unstable as long as the major centers can overleap it for direct attack upon each other; but if their potential hostilities can be worked out only through local operations of a police-force type, the frontiers are likely to become as stable as those in Latin America.

The demilitarized world will thus start with a great-power *détente* and a general reduction of armaments everywhere to a police-force level. What is striking about this assumed situation is the very large measure of stability it will contain. It is often argued that even general and complete disarmament cannot abolish war; even if all nuclear weapons are destroyed, this will not eliminate from the human brain the knowledge of how to rebuild them; even if all military forces are reduced to lightly armed police, they will go on fighting each other (even with "sticks and stones") as did the little armies of the seventeenth and eighteenth centuries, with nothing more than their smoothbore muskets. What this totally overlooks is the rapidly developing change in the international power structure that both makes demilitarization a possibility and will tend to conserve it once it is achieved. It is, of course, impossible to eradicate the knowledge of how to make nuclear bombs; it is not impossible to inculcate the realization that it is pointless to make them. The knowledge of how to revive a war system will remain; it is any reason for doing so that will disappear, as it has already begun to disappear today.

The stability of a demilitarized world would resemble the present stabilization of Western Europe under NATO much more than the attempted stabilization of Europe under the war system after 1918. The power organization of the modern world has in fact progressed enormously—taking the globe as a whole, there is actually more "law and order" and less violence in it than ever before in human history—and for a demilitarized future one need not posit the relatively primitive power organization that made wars frequent in Latin America in the nineteenth century and incessant in Western Europe in the eighteenth and seventeenth centuries. In a demilitarized world each of the four or five highly stabilized great-power governments would be committed, not simply in regard to each other but with their own peoples and taxpayers, to the abolition of war. In each, the large fraction of the Gross National Product now going into war and the war industries would have been converted to other and more desirable uses. The economic costs of a rearmament policy would appear to all of them to be enormous—especially when police arrangements had eliminated any need for it—while the risks it would entail would seem wholly incommensurate with any end that could probably be attained by it, much as the political-military risks of actually resorting to nuclear arsenals today seem incommensurate with anything that could thereby be gained. When Hitler launched Germany on the paths of rearmament and military "power," there were probably few if any Germans who thought the objectives were mistaken; today, a new Hitler would be excoriated in his own country first of all, and in a generally demilitarized international society this would be true in all countries. In many states today the leaders are those who benefit in power and wealth from the war system; in a world demilitarized, the leaders would be those who had benefited from the process of demilitarization, who were committed to it and who would be the first to denounce any effort at its revival.

The four or five great stabilized, industrialized, and self-integrated power centers in fact offer a firm foundation on which to construct a demilitarized world power structure. If they were all, the problem would perhaps have been solved by now. But beyond their borders perhaps a third of the human race is found in the "uncommitted" or "underdeveloped" or "neutralist" world. That either the Western democratic-capitalist system or the Sino-Soviet Communist system can wholly or successfully organize this vast segment of humanity, with all its complex internal power issues, seems most unlikely. The "domination of the world" is as ephemeral a bogey for one side as for the other; and if the "cold war" has indicated anything it has indicated that "world domination" is as far beyond the power of the Soviet-Communist system as it is beyond the power of Western "capitalism." The comparative disorganization of the "uncommitted world" will doubtless continue to invite the great-power centers to rivalry for influence and control over its development. But rivalry need not, as the "cold war" again suggests, take the form of organized war. The great-power organizations themselves cannot be assumed to have been fixed for all eternity. One must expect conflict of interest, with resultant change and flux both within the great-power systems and among them, as well as in the uncommitted areas; and one must, we believe, expect a fair amount of riot, local violence, and guerrilla war in the process. In a generally demilitarized world such episodes need be no more disruptive to the underlying power balance on which the demilitarization rests than was, for example, the Irish guerrilla war for independence against Great Britain. But to keep such problems within limits, it already seems necessary for the demilitarized world to develop at least a minimal form of supranational authority.

The necessity, not merely for an international but for a genuinely supranational authority, has long been felt; and men have restlessly looked for its source in many places, from the "collective security" of the League of Nations down to "world opinion" or "moral authority," or a development of "natural law," uniformly without avail. We have many international authorities, but few sources of supranational authority have become available to us. Of course, the time may come when it is derived from a genuinely supranational global government, exercising over all states and groups and individuals within them powers, backed by a global "monopoly of force," comparable to those exercised by the federal government over the American states and their individual citizens. Until that obviously far distant time, it is believed that where supranational authority is needed, it can be derived only from the principle that underlay the United Nations charter—the principle of great-power unanimity.

In the United Nations charter it was hoped to secure great-power unanimity through the device of the great-power veto. This did not work. A supranational authority, if it is to be an *authority* at all, must be veto-free within the limits of its empowerment. The avenue to unanimity is not to be found through a veto, but through limiting the empowerment strictly to those areas in which all parties will recognize that it is to their own interest to accept what is in effect compulsory jurisdiction. In designing a demilitarized world, the question is what is the very minimum of supranational authority that it will necessitate. It is believed that this minimum, given the existing power structure in the world, can be put at a very modest level.

Once the world has been demilitarized, supranational authority will be needed primarily to ensure that rearmament does not take place; that the national police forces do not gradually develop into military threats against each other; and to exert in the less stable areas of the globe the kind of police power the UN has already been called upon to supply in Palestine and Africa. That it would have to establish compulsory enforceable jurisdiction in the settlement of "disputes" between the great powers seems doubtful. Once the enormous weapons systems, with the fears and the insoluble issues of abstract power that surround them, have been eliminated, differences that will continue to arise between the great-power centers will surely be susceptible to resolution by existing negotiatory and arbitral processes, as they are now within the Western community.

For all these purposes the supranational authority will have a modicum of armed force under its own veto-free command. It would not need and could not have a great supranational nuclear military force capable of coercing any of the great states—upon whose assent its own existence and effectiveness would depend. The whole success of a demilitarized world turns upon the *abolition* of military coercion as a means of adjusting the relations of states, and one cannot hope to abolish it on the national level if one is simply to reassemble it on the international level. The international police force, which appears in all plans for disarmament, must be just that—a police force and not an army. In the prevention of rearmament, most of the political and psychological factors will be, as has been suggested, on the side of the authority, and its useful instruments will be those of investigation, intelligence, and report, not of armed might. Once the world has been demilitarized, it is believed that it will be possible to define certain kinds of incitations or conspiracies looking toward clandestine rearmament or weapons development as international crimes, and to give the supranational police rights to intervene against such actions similar to those the American federal police organs enjoy within the several states. But by and large the great, highly organized powers can be relied upon to police themselves, as we now rely, for example, upon the great powers in NATO.

The functions and empowerment of the supranational police in the less stable areas of the globe are less easy to envisage. Since Theodore Roosevelt's claim to a "police power" in the Caribbean, if not long before, the idea of an international, or at least great-state, police control over "the little bandit nations" has been prominent in the discourse; but it has never been logically developed, and attempts to give it practical expression have rarely been happy. Khrushchev has cavalierly cut through the dilemma by saying that it will be the function of the international police to prevent all wars "except those of national liberation." The indignation with which this has been received in the West conceals the fact that the West (unless it really proposes to establish an iron *status quo* upon the globe) has no better answer for the riots, rebellions, and guerrilla wars that would be fairly certain to continue in a world generally demilitarized. Where the limits of supranational authority (and supranational armed power) in such situations are likely to lie is a problem that calls for much more study than it has been given.

One can only say that we have, on the one hand, been learning by experience (for proof one need only compare the "UN police action" in Korea with those in Palestine and the Congo); while, on the other hand, the problem of local violence, rebellion, and guerrilla war will lose much of its dangerous significance in a generally demilitarized world. Local power conflicts may be anything but bloodless (though we tend to forget how many problems have been solved since 1945, how many vast changes have been effected, by substantially bloodless means) and may, as in Algeria or the Congo, present appalling pictures of injustice, cruelty, and disorder. But they are not "causes" of major war; they can at most only trigger a major war already prepared by other military and power factors. The notion that armed violence or even small-scale international war anywhere represents a kind of center of infection, capable, unless immediately suppressed, of spreading into a Third World War, stands the real processes of international politics on their head. The small war cannot explode into a great one unless the great one already stands ready for detonation. The small war is like the dynamite cap. The dynamite cap is in itself by no means harmless, and has to be handled with care to avoid local damage. But unless and until the dynamite is attached to it, the damage will remain localized.

For the time being, at least, the great powers have been effectively demilitarized by their own weaponry; a great war seems as of today impracticable, and is not in preparation. The great powers have eschewed direct military intervention in African issues, and the police problem has fallen more or less by default to the UN. The forces it has deployed are very small; they have not attempted to resolve the political and power issues involved, but have mainly tried only to limit the violence. This situation, it would seem, would be the same whether the great powers are temporarily demilitarized by fear of their own weaponry or permanently demilitarized by a *détente* and disarmament. The working results, in the Congo and elsewhere, have been disagreeable in the extreme; but they have not been catastrophic. It is hard to doubt that this experience provides a model for the probable function of a supranational police force in dealing with the remaining violence in a world generally disarmed.

The demilitarized world will not and cannot eliminate the infinite variety of power struggles inherent in the nature of man. What it can and must do is to eliminate the war system, under which all these struggles "head up," both needlessly and catastrophically, into a giant military struggle between four or five great centers of organized power. Mortal combat (especially mortal combat raised to levels of mass destruction hitherto practiced only in the ancient world) is not the only, it is not the usual, and it is not the final or even effective test of power in the modern world. There are many other ways besides organized war available today for resolving the almost infinite variety of power issues with which humanity must struggle. It is impossible to say with any precision just how these many issues would be dealt with in the absence of the great weapons systems; it is not impossible to prophecy that they would be dealt with much better than the weapons systems are likely to do. It is enough, for the moment, to point to the essential viability of a global system built upon the four or five great national power centers that now exist, these being mutually demilitarized to police-force levels and provided with a modicum of supranational force to ensure that no remilitarization took place and to provide for at least a minimum of order in the less stable areas of the world.

In many discussions of international peace, the "sovereign state" appears as the great villain in the drama. But this is to overlook what a really remarkable achievement in human organization the great modern industrial state—like the United States, the Soviet Union, the Western democracies, and potentially Communist China—really is. Its contributions toward human productivity and welfare are immense; so are its potential contributions toward peace and a reasonably just order. It is true that in its Communist and Western forms it has arisen out of somewhat different historical backgrounds; the two enshrine different concepts of "freedom"; the justice of one is not the justice of the other. Both have, however, proved themselves operable ways in which to organize the infinite variety of men in creative cooperation. Their rise has already brought to the world as a whole a far greater measure of "law and order" with far less actual violence or bloodshed than history has ever previously known. The world as it exists today is a tolerable one—"better" by most standards than any that previously existed—and it is only the fears of what the great weapons systems will do to it in the future that prevent our cheerful acceptance of the modern power structure.

Here is a large measure of working world organization already attained. If the great power centers can refrain from tearing each other to radioactive rubble, they can become in themselves an adequate base for a world system that, while not perfect, not static, not completely nonviolent, can, with only small additions to the institutional arrangements we now have, work at least far better than the war system ever has toward the betterment of man.

CHAPTER SEVEN

THE NECESSARY
REVOLUTION

"THE EASIEST THING TO DO ABOUT WORLD ORDER," AS HARVEY Wheeler has observed, "is to prove that it is politically impossible." The imagined picture of a world order from which war has been eliminated seems reasonable, workable, not too demanding of a fallible human nature, and likely to be self-reinforcing. It will be objected immediately, however, that it is also totally impossible of realization. It is pure Utopianism. How are you going to secure the initial great-power *détente* that it demands? How are you going to be sure that the Russians really intend peace rather than war? How are you going to induce the Chinese to disarm or in any other way support a warless system when they seem committed to the view that another great war is inevitable? How, once we have divested ourselves of any possibility of resort to war, can we secure the safety and vital power positions of the Western democratic-capitalist system? The picture may be attractive, but, it will be said, it is wholly visionary.

In a sense the charge is true and cannot be avoided. The picture is Utopian because it is also revolutionary; and all revolutions—great or small, political, economic, or technological—always appear to be impractical until they have occurred. They require men to alter in some respects their ways of doing things, their habits of thought, their concepts of what is due and just in men's relations with one another. What "is not done," and therefore, by every lesson of experience, "impossible" before the revolution becomes the accepted commonplace of thought and behavior after the revolution has been effected. "A disarmed world," as Charles D. Bolton has put it, "is as inconceivable to most people today as was a world without an hereditary ruling class to our mediaeval ancestors."[1] Today no one, except possibly in some of the more backward parts of the world, sees anything "impossible" about getting along without an hereditary ruling class; such a device seems no longer necessary to the unity, the internal order, or security of the nation-state. It once fulfilled highly important social functions—without it, it may be said, modern society could never have come into being—but alternative ways of discharging these functions have developed, and today the hereditary ruling class is a picturesque anachronism. The dynastic, marital, and religious problems of the hereditary sovereigns were once matters of intense interest to their peoples; today they no longer matter. The interna-

[1] "What the Peace Movement Needs," *The Nation*, January 27, 1962.

tional political system that surrounded their persons and their personal problems has disappeared, and because other modes for dealing with international relations have developed, men no longer think or act in this respect as they did in the seventeenth century.

The charge of Utopianism, when brought against the demilitarized world, is thus not final; the "impossible" of one era repeatedly becomes the commonplace of the succeeding one. But neither is the answer Utopists are accustomed to bringing when their ideal systems are challenged. It is insufficient to say, as they often do, that if only men would believe and act as their new world requires, there would be no problem about bringing it into being. The practical Utopist (or practical revolutionary) must operate on a narrower plane. He cannot expect men as they are to adopt his system out of hand, neither can he wait for them to turn into angels. If he is a realist he must, it is believed, ask himself two questions: To what minimum extent must established patterns of thought and behavior be modified in order to make my Utopia practical and workable? How can these minimal changes be brought about, or how can one expect them to come about?

The broad change in contemporary habits of thought and action required to make a demilitarized world possible can be rather simply summed up. It is merely that men everywhere should come to regard the war system—the system, that is, of organized war between the great modern power centers—as obsolete. This may seem to say less than that men should come to regard it as criminal or pathological or

ultimately catastrophic; actually it is to say a good deal
more. Most men already regard war as criminal or pathologic
or ultimately catastrophic; but this has not helped us much
with the war problem. As war comes to be regarded as
irrelevant, the problem will approach solution. The criminal
or pathological or catastrophic elements in our affairs are
never irrelevant; by attaching such adjectives to them we
proclaim our intense belief in their importance. In ancient
societies (the same is true of modern ones as well) the violation of certain taboos was a major crime, and the enormity
of the crime measured the importance the society attached to
the observance of the taboo. With the passage of time and
the changes in the cultural patterns, many taboos became
obsolete. Their violation no longer seemed to matter, and the
violation itself ceased to be criminal. As long as we look on
war as a crime it will doubtless remain with us, in spite of
Nuremberg trials and arguments over "war guilt." When we
see the whole system as obsolete and useless, organized war
will begin to go the way of the hereditary ruling class, or any
other of the many human institutions and cultural patterns
that have outlived their usefulness.

Unfortunately, for men to come to regard organized war
as obsolete requires more drastic changes in cultural patterns
and thought habits than for them to see it as criminal or
pathological. The broad change subsumes many more specific
ones. Men must, for example, abandon their habit of believing
that the safety and survival of the national community
depend upon its military power and military preparations.
We already know that this is not the case—that massive

accumulations of military power in a nuclear age are far more likely to destroy than to conserve the national community. But we have as yet been unable to bring ourselves to *believe* this. Most of us are still unable to grasp the fact that the senseless question, "Would you rather be Red or dead?" is indeed senseless. It permits of no answer because its terms correspond to nothing in the contemporary international world; it has a purely emotional impact upon us because it summons up ideas or notions about the way in which the international world operates that are completely erroneous. It is senseless here; corresponding questions when asked in Russia or China are equally senseless, and men everywhere must alter their ideas to the extent necessary for them to realize it.

Men must abandon the idea that the surviving military institutions in one great state are in themselves a direct threat to other states. They must, to put it in another way, come to realize that the Soviet megaton bombs are as useless, in the long run, to the Soviet state as our own megaton bombs are to us. This realization is amply sustainable from the actual history of the past fifteen years, and seems to be more and more clearly demonstrable in events as time goes on. As the conclusion more clearly emerges, it will permit us and the other great military powers to make considerably greater contributions toward eventual demilitarization than we seem able to do now. We do not believe that we can now practically, or perhaps even safely, embark upon complete unilateral disarmament. We might, as was earlier suggested, go a good deal further in bowing out of the arms race than we now dare to do. We could accept test bans or similar disarmament beginnings on a much lower level of inspection and verification than we now feel it necessary to demand. If the institution is really, in our minds, obsolete and meaningless, one need take correspondingly lesser precautions against its possible revival—not, it must once more be insisted, because we come to "trust" the Russians or the Chinese but because we see no advantage to them in reviving it.

There are other established concepts that men must be willing to surrender if a demilitarized world is to be achieved. One of the most important, probably, is the myth of organized war as essential to the unity, the purpose, the "soul" of the state. We now believe that men must be willing to die for the state if the state is to survive ("Would you rather be Red or dead?"), just as it was once believed that they had to be willing to die at the stake for their religion if truth was to prevail. The great apparatus of military ritual, of the military uniform, of obeisance to the flag, of military training and obedience, is thought to be essential to the maintenance of a national unity and purpose—and it is thought that these must be sealed by the possibility of blood sacrifice if they are to retain their magical social power. In any society, democratic or dictatorial, the army remains the highest, most solemn expression of dedication to the common purpose, and many nation-states today, which find themselves under no significant external threat whatever, are reluctant to abandon military establishments that serve so many purposes of internal cohesion. Yet there are several smaller ones that have done so, without adverse result; and the argument ignores the successful history of other modern states that have not for decades or even centuries been involved in war.

Men must abandon the idea that either the great nuclear arsenals or the huge conventional military establishments maintained in the great power centers—the United States and Western Europe, Russia, China—are going to affect very greatly the future of world history. At the cost of untold agony and loss of life, we have now reached a position in which about two-thirds of the inhabitants of the world live in these four or five stabilized political-social organizations, each well ordered, largely self-sufficient, self-confident, and each incapable of seriously affecting the destiny of the others through warfare except at the price of suicide. Of these two-thirds of the globe's peoples, one is organized on mainly Western-democratic lines and the other on mainly Communist lines. Whether the masses in the "free world" are, on balance, happier or more productive or more content with their lot than the masses in the "unfree" world seems a somewhat academic question. But one thing can be said with certainty. That is, that neither the megaton arsenals nor the tank divisions are going to resolve such questions. Two world wars succeeded in churning up the human organization of the globe as it existed in 1910, with results which were in some ways beneficial as well as lamentable. A third war holds out no hope of any beneficial results whatever. A third world war can produce a universal catastrophe; short of that, the material needs, the political relations, the ambitions of the great power centers are not going to be significantly affected by their military establishments; war of this kind is already obsolete, and must sooner or later be recognized to be so.

There remains another third of the global population, more or less, in a state of relative instability, change, and revolution. In their efforts to control or channel developments in this huge area, the relatively stable great-power centers are in rivalry. They are not, it must be insisted, in a state of war (the "cold war" has always been a misleading analogy), and their weaponry is unlikely to be of much effect. The great powers have not in fact deployed their armaments in this area since 1945. Even in Korea, the closest approach during this period to a resort to the organized war system, the United States used only a small fraction of its total military power. The fourfold increase in 1950 in the American military budget went for the most part toward averting the supposed danger of a war in Europe, not toward winning the actual war in Korea. The position was strikingly different from that presented by the Russo-Japanese War of 1904–1905, in which both sides really strained themselves to the limit to achieve a conventional military victory.

In Indochina and in Algeria the French may have committed a relatively greater proportion of their military resources to victory; in neither case, however, did they make a total commitment comparable to that of 1914 or 1939, while these were both guerrilla wars in which "victory" on the old pattern was essentially impossible. "The object of war," as General MacArthur (in one of his many moods) once sonorously declared, "is victory." This was roughly true of the war system as it operated in Western international relations through the past three centuries. Recognizable, clear-cut "victory" was as essential to the successful working of the system as accountable money profits are essential to the operation of a capitalist economic system. "Victory," accepted by both contestants, was the key to the whole business. But guerrilla war is fundamentally a denial that military victory matters—it is a denial of the very idea of victory; and the fact that wherever, since 1945, armed violence has significantly affected the social, political, and power relations of peoples it has almost exclusively taken the form of guerrilla warfare is one of the more striking of our demonstrations of the obsolescence of the organized war system.

It will never, presumably, be possible to eliminate armed violence, with its concomitants of manslaughter, from human affairs. What does seem possible, and indeed probable, is the elimination of the ritual organization of violence into forms that seem to ensure the slaughter of men by the tens or hundreds of millions. In considering this possibility, the resurgence of mob violence and guerrilla warfare as effective (if in themselves far from pretty) modes in the adjustment of international group relations is of the utmost interest. Guerrilla war has seldom, if ever, ended in anything like a recognizable "victory" on the old pattern. The outcome may register shifts in power, often very great shifts in power, but usually has the appearance of a compromise rather than of "victory." Guerrilla wars may succeed (as in Ireland in the 1920's) or fail (as in the Philippines after 1899), but whatever the outcome they usually leave an effect upon the future that it is difficult to describe by either the term "victory" or "defeat." They observe discernible laws that do not apply to the great organized conflicts between highly armed states. These laws are only beginning to receive the attention they deserve.

Regarded as a form of politics, there are two aspects of guerrilla war that are of particular interest. One is that it cannot survive unless it has behind it a large measure of popular support. In this, it represents a kind of crude popular referendum; but how far the affirmative "votes" are given because of hope, because of fear, because of terror, is usually as obscure as are the reasons why affirmative votes are given in more sophisticated electoral processes. The other interesting aspect of guerrilla war is the fact that it usually cannot succeed without outside support. Normally, it must have outside sources of money and weapons, safe bases for recruitment, training, and hospitalization of casualties. While the rule may not be invariable, there are many instances to sustain it. Perhaps it is enough to compare Cuba's ten-year "War of Independence" in 1868–1878, which failed because no one outside was greatly interested in it, with the second war for independence, which, beginning in 1895, succeeded brilliantly because of the immense emotional, logistic, and finally military support the United States put behind it.

In the first aspect, guerrilla war represents something like a popular referendum. In the second aspect, unhappily, it represents something like a vicarious great-power contest. As we ought to realize by now, it is not just the Russians or the Chinese who back their own sides in such contests; the United States and other Western powers have long been accustomed to doing the same. In the less stable areas of the world, guerrilla war is likely to represent *both* a popular referendum and a great-nation power conflict. It is hard to separate the values involved. The fact appears to remain, however, that the results yielded by power contests of this kind are normally accepted as final both for the internal power struggle they represent and for the external great-power struggle that may be at issue. It is today the settled policy of the United States to provide the South Vietnamese with all the logistic and advisory support they may be able to use, but not to try to fight their war for them. Unless the Vietnamese can save themselves from the Communist pressure, the United States will not try to save them on its own initiative. What this seems to imply is that whereas the issue of Western as against Communist control of South Vietnam is important, it is not important enough for a major war and not so important that it cannot be left to decision by the complex factors on the ground. As a means of "saving" South Vietnam from Communism, the major-war system is obsolete; but the issue itself is not so tragic that it cannot reasonably be left to the lesser instrumentalities of power that are available.

To say, as has been said above, that men must abandon the idea that the existing hypertrophied armaments of the great powers are going to affect the future history of the world materially is to say that they must come to understand that there are alternative ways in which the world's power struggles can be (as they are being) conducted. They must come to realize that neither the thermonuclear holocaust itself nor the continued threat of it is in any way essential to a reasonably viable and rational adjustment of the world's power problems. To accept this is not to condemn the demilitarized world to an endless succession of guerrilla "wars of liberation" or violent riots, competitively fomented by the stable powers. The rise of mob violence and guerrilla war in the contemporary world is only one way in which the immensely complex problems of power are being resolved. It is in only rather small areas of the world, after all, that violence of this kind is significant in international affairs today; in a world demilitarized to police-force levels, the power problems themselves are certain to take on different forms. For the present argument, it is enough to say that for the demilitarized world to come into existence, men everywhere must come to regard the massive nuclear and conventional military establishments of the great states as irrelevant to the real problems of power.

To change men's minds and attitudes in all these ways may seem to sum up to a very large order, indeed. It means nothing less than an elimination of the myth system that men now apply to international relations in favor of a more practicable, less disastrous myth system. This, it is often said, is impossible, since men live and probably always will live by the myths they construct. But nothing is more familiar in our experience than the fact that the myths are changeable. The ancients very seriously believed that natural disaster could be averted only by propitiatory sacrifice to the gods. Proper ritual and punctually performed sacrifice were as necessary to ancient statesmanship as our own (financial) sacrifices to the multimegaton bomb or the super-ready warning system are to statesmanship today. An Aztec leader would have been derelict in his duty to his people if he had refrained from slaughtering captives by the thousand on the bloody teocalli of Mexico; much as the humane and rational men who were running the First World War would have thought themselves criminal if they had refrained from laying a generation of European youth in windrows under the enemy machine guns. We no longer believe that animal or human sacrifice is relevant to averting natural disaster. It does not seem impossible that we shall come to believe that the slaughter of human beings by the million is irrelevant to the solution of the political-economic problems of an integrated global society.

Two centuries ago there were probably few men who believed that a Western European society could survive and prosper without the support of hellfire. Even the skeptics who had begun to doubt the evidence for eternal torment, at least as it applied to themselves, would have feared to remove the notion from the catechisms and the textbooks. If men generally ceased to believe in the possibility of eternal damnation, how could an even approximately moral and God-fearing community be held together? The inquisitors who burned heretics at the stake carried the idea to a logical, indeed, scientific, conclusion, which reminds one of some scientific reasoning that can be heard today. It was better and more humane to inflict a half-hour of excruciating torture upon a body if one thereby saved the soul from an eternity of torture imagined as of the same excruciating kind.

Modern scientists like Edward Teller or scientific thinkers like Herman Kahn may be skeptical about their own condemnation to the hellfire of nuclear war, but feel it essential to the health of the society that it *believe* in nuclear hellfire and act accordingly. And while they hope (as, no doubt, did the inquisitors) that this policy will avert the damnation of the human race, they are quite prepared to incinerate half the world if that is necessary to prevent if from falling into the Communist heresy. Today hellfire, in the old-fashioned sense of eternal and excruciating damnation, plays no great part in social or political life. The myth has lost its credibility, and insofar as it lingers at all has been sublimated into more spiritual and philosophical concepts of the "torture of the damned." It does not seem impossible that the terrifying myths of the great weapons systems may undergo a similar sublimation.

There are other examples of revolutionary changes in the myth systems, more directly associated with politics, and more apropos. Most thoughtful Americans had come by 1860 to a realization that the institution of chattel slavery was an anachronism, almost certain of extinction in time. But the rather complex myth systems that had come by that time to surround it—myth systems relating to private property, states' rights, racial supremacy, political and economic power within the Union—had combined to render its abolition impossible. In this instance it took a great war to shatter the myth systems and rebuild others in which abolition was not only possible but indeed virtually automatic. It is interesting that even late in the second year of the war Lincoln did not feel that he could achieve the "impossible" end of abolishing the institution of slavery itself. The Emancipation Proclamation was a war measure; it applied only to slaves in rebel territory, and those who were freed under its terms were commonly referred to as "contrabands." They were not men freed because all men have a right to "Life, Liberty and the pursuit of Happiness," but a military resource—almost a military raw material—denied to an adversary on the same grounds that one denies him any other military resource in time of war. The rules that govern the capture of "contraband" at sea in time of war in no way invalidate the institution of private property or the rights normally attaching to it; and the Emancipation Proclamation in no way invalidated the institution of chattel slavery—at least ostensibly. In fact, of course, when the war was over the institution had been abolished; and the Thirteenth Amendment, an impossible enactment in 1861, had become not only possible but unavoidable by 1865.

In this case, the agonies of war had changed the preexisting myth system, or at least rendered its modification inescapable. There are other cases in which the functions of war or military violence are more obscure. Jesse D. Clarkson suggests in his recent analysis [2] that the Russian Revolution began with Alexander II's emancipation of the serfs in 1861. At that time, the whole Russian social, political, and economic system had become an anachronism. The myths that supported the autocracy, the new bureaucracy, the small bourgeoisie, the landowning boyars, and the institution of serfdom were

[2] *A History of Russia* (New York: Random House, 1962).

inconsistent with each other and with the social and economic requirements of the state. To Alexander's advisers it seemed necessary to abolish the institution of serfdom, primarily in order to provide a landowning and therefore conservative peasantry as a foundation upon which the autocracy and its bureaucrats could face the bourgeoisie and the boyars. A change in the myth system was necessary. It was easy enough to write and promulgate the Emancipation Proclamation. But the existing myth system—again concerning, property rights, feudal rights, liberties, protections—rendered this more or less nugatory. In attempting to respect all the established claims to property rights and power, the "reform" really reformed almost nothing; it was often bitterly resisted by the peasants themselves as depriving them of securities with no corresponding freedoms, and Russia continued to resist the modernization that was becoming increasingly essential. The myth system surrounding serfdom in 1861 was too strong for an Emancipation Proclamation to produce the results expected from it. But from that time on the myth system was subject to an erosion that pointed steadily to its ultimate disappearance. Not a few students (of whom Clarkson is one) believe that a "constitutionalization" of the anachronistic Russian autocracy was unavoidable and would have come in time, *except* for the disastrous effects of the First World War. Under the staggering blows of this foreign conflict the Russian social, economic, political, and military system collapsed before it could be reformed. Somebody had to seize power; the Bolsheviks did so, and violently swept away every element in the old myth system that obstructed them, setting up a wholly different system of myths that has since endured. If, however, it is true that in the absence of the First World War the czarist Russian system would have undergone modification (as happened in nineteenth century Britain) to adjust to the new conditions, it is unnecessary to conclude that cultural and conceptual patterns can be changed only through violent revolution of the most extreme kind.

Technological revolution can have effects as drastic as those of political revolution on established myth systems, but they usually become manifest more gradually and without violence. The rise, and subsequent passing, of the steam-powered, coal-burning technology in Britain had enormous effects upon both the internal and external power relations of the British people—upon their "world power," upon their internal class relationships, upon the nature and control of private property, upon the power relationships of the British elite—but all occurred without any great violence; and if the foreign wars in which they engaged were of effect in the process, it was (as in the case of Russia) a peripheral effect on the great internal power issues, agonizing and destructive though it may have been for the people of Britain.

Men can and do constantly change their concepts, their ruling myth systems, under the impact of experience, of technological change, of outward circumstance. Things impossible to one age become the commonplaces of the next; and while it seems that, too often, violence and bloodshed have been catalysts in the process, they are not always necessary and have by no means always been present. If as a consequence of our existing myth systems concerning power, property rights, and international relations our Western democratic-capitalist society is wrecked in a thermonuclear war (as czarist Russian society was wrecked in the First World War), there can be little doubt that some dictator will arise to impose a new myth system upon it, or upon what may remain of it. But it does not seem at all impossible that without such a catastrophe our myths may undergo modification into forms that will render the catastrophe unnecessary and improbable.

What has to be done—or has to come about—is well illuminated by Thomas C. Schelling's work on total disarmament.[3] Schelling is an exponent of the school that holds that even total disarmament cannot prevent war: "Short of universal brain surgery," he observes, "nothing can erase the memory of weapons and how to build them." Even in a disarmed world, "*if* war breaks out a nation can rearm unless its capacity is destroyed at the outset." As long as these ideas are governing, we can obviously get nowhere. Schelling tells us that as we advance toward general disarmament we must cling to our military deterrents. "Prudence" (which seems a rather odd word under the circumstances) tells us not to step off the train of military security until it has come to a full stop. But this really begs the question. Prudence may equally instruct us to make a wild leap for the embankment if we find ourselves on a train rushing out of control down a long grade to certain disaster. As long as we continue to

[3] "The Role of Deterrence in Total Disarmament," *Foreign Affairs*, April, 1962.

regard war as an uncontrollable natural calamity, and must base our policies upon guesses as to what would happen "if" it "breaks out," we shall remain mired in the eighteenth century international myth systems, peopled by all the gods and demons, controllable only by incantation and sacrifice, of Tom Paine's "system of war and expence." Wars do not in fact just "break out"; they are made by men and can be unmade by men. The task is not to construct policies that will be successful *if* war breaks out; it is to construct policies that will assure that war does not and cannot break out. Such policies are now quite clearly within the grasp of modern statesmanship. In the modern world, major war is no longer simply a natural calamity, avertible by appropriate sacrifices to the gods of nationalism or genuflections before the multi-megaton bombs, which may have a more terrible physical reality than the gods after which so many of them are named —Ajax, Nike, Zeus, and the rest—but are as helpless to save us. We must cease erecting into "powers" factors—like "air power" or "nuclear power" or "sea power"—which are as powerless to preserve or deliver us as were the vague "powers" to which men once prayed and by which they swore. We must come to realize that the problem of armed violence in our ordered and integrated world is essentially a police, and not a military, problem.

This we must do; and if we are to look forward to a de-militarized world we can do no less. We cannot stand on plans for general disarmament, for test bans, for United Nations revision, even for massive investment in the under-developed countries. These things may prove of great value, but all are secondary. Unless we can revise the basic international myth system, they will be of little effect. To the extent to which the myth system is revised, they will become practicable and helpful. The task is to secure the revision of the myth system. It is a difficult task; it is not an impossible one.

It has been argued above that President Kennedy might well have taken a different position than he did on the nuclear test ban. At least one reason why he did not was his fear of the popular reaction: popular attitudes, which is to say the ruling myths, simply would not permit it. But the attitudes have been changing, and will, it is believed, continue to do so. There are many moves in international relations possible to an American President today that would have been quite out of the question only five or ten years ago. It is the responsibility of the vocal public to provide the rational thinking and argument that will encourage such changes; it is the responsibility of the President and other world leaders to promote them all by the many instrumentalities that are available to their hands.

We live in an international world to which hypertrophied military force is largely irrelevant. But our myth systems clustering about international relations will not permit us to believe this. It is, of course, true that general disarmament could not eradicate the knowledge of how to rebuild the weapons systems; but it could make their rebuilding seem useless to everyone. According to Herman Kahn, the knowledge of how to build a "Doomsday Machine" exists today; but actually to build one seems pointless (as well as fearfully dangerous) to everyone, including Kahn. Once the world has managed to rid itself of the existing, semi-doomsday machines, their reconstruction would be equally pointless, because of the modification in the ruling myth systems that this would bring about. The abolition of war cannot be brought about by any juggling with the great weaponry itself; it can come about through an alteration in the myth systems that now surround and sustain the weapons. But how?

CHAPTER EIGHT

THE PROBLEM
OF POWER

How do you make a revolution—or how does a revolution come about—of the magnitude implied by such a reordering of the international myth system? What is involved here is not, as is often said, the establishment of a radically new "world order" so much as the modification or rearrangement of the very high degree of world order we already possess. It is an order that supplies—as does any social order—a structuring of the complex and multitudinous power relations of those who live under it, which in this case includes the population of the globe. Much of the time and for most of these peoples it does so with a rather surprising minimum of violence (by comparison with any previous age) and without resort to major organized war. But the structuring has so developed in the present century as to make not only a major war but a human catastrophe seem ultimately unavoidable.

Our question may be rephrased: How can our ideas about power and with them the international power structure be so modified as to avert this result?

Unless one can somehow grapple with our ideas about power itself, specific or institutional answers seem not to be enough. Clark and Sohn's thoughtful and ingenious plan [1] for revision of the United Nations Charter, for example, is bound to seem unrealistic unless one assumes a transformation of existing myth systems concerning power on the international stage. And unless one can form some theory as to how the myth systems might change, both plans for the future and extrapolations from the past have little validity.

Power, admittedly, is a difficult and elusive subject. Many highly capable minds have debated it; the word appears to correspond to something quite actual and precise in human affairs, yet it has never received really satisfactory definition. The concept of "power" is as changeable, as much subject to various and contradictory definitions, as the concept of "freedom," with which it is closely connected. We usually think of "freedom" as the ability to choose as we will; we usually think of "power" as the ability to induce others to choose as we wish them to do. We know that "power," like "freedom," is never absolute; even very great power may be surrounded by very great limitations. In the ordinary affairs of life these rather simple concepts may work well enough. It is easy to say that a holdup man's pistol gives him the power to cause his victim to choose to hand over the wallet; though

[1] *World Peace Through World Law* (Cambridge, Mass.: Harvard University Press, 1960).

it is a power limited by the stubbornness of the victim and the possible proximity of the police. We can say, perhaps with less assurance, that an industrialist's command of large economic resources gives him the power, through his price and wage policies, to cause great numbers of people of whom he has never heard to make economic choices; though the power is limited by the fact (among other things) that the choices may not be those he had planned or even desired. The political power of the American Presidency enables the incumbent to induce thousands or millions of people to make choices that in sum may (or may not) conduce to results the incumbent believes will contribute to the common good. And so the game may be carried on. But as one gets into ever greater complexities of groups, states, and nations, with ever greater vagueness as to the nature of the powers involved and the real extent of the limitations surrounding them, the attempt to abstract a generalized idea of "power" as a force in human affairs becomes more and more difficult. The highly integrated modern state, for example, finds itself disposing of a colossal military "power" under conditions severely inhibiting its use. What does the military "power" really signify?

Under the circumstances, "power" is a concept difficult to capture and even more difficult to apply to the affairs of the modern world. There are some who see not only organized international war but group conflict in general as explicable in terms of an abstract "power conflict" rather simply conceived. In this version, when there is a wide disparity in "power" between two groups, no problem arises. The weaker is unable to challenge the stronger, and does not attempt to do so; the stronger is unafraid of the weaker, and sees no reason to prepare the latter's destruction. The case of the United States and Canada is often cited here. However, as two military states tend to approach equality of power the tensions, it is said, begin to rise. It has even been suggested, rather naïvely, that by projecting with modern calculating machines the changing elements of "power" in the United States and the Soviet Union, it would be possible to predict the time of approaching equality and therefore of maximum tension and probable war.

One difficulty with this is, of course, that of weighting and projecting the several elements of "power." Even if "military power" alone is being considered, one is still involved in all sorts of incomparables, such as steel productive capacity, available population, and so on, as well as with the weaponry. A somewhat subtler view relates both war and other forms of conflict not to relative levels of "power," but to shifts in preexisting power relations. Two roughly equivalent powers may remain at peace, no matter how high the absolute powers are built, as long as the power relationship remains static. It is when the power of one is tending to decline and that of the other tending to rise that war must result; the declining power must fight in order to avert further decline; the rising power must fight in order that its rise be not interrupted.

Many have supported this view; A. J. P. Taylor carries it so far as to say that all modern wars have been "preventive wars," and probably most of the greater wars can be called so. It still seems an unsatisfactorily simplistic theory. Harvey Wheeler [2] has given it a further refinement. In this view, a war or any other group power struggle does not so much produce the basic shift in power relationships as simply register or record a shift that has already taken place; the violence of the war or the severity of the political power struggle serves simply to demonstrate the fact of the new power relationships, to render them acceptable to all, and to establish the new myth systems necessary to support them. To take a revolutionary but non military example, one might cite the fierce political battles in Great Britain in 1910 and 1911 that led to the Parliament Act of 1911. This effectively destroyed the political power of the House of Lords, and with it that of the hereditary aristocracy. A conventional view would be that it was the battle and the Parliament Act that effected the revolution. But one could also say that the revolution had in fact occurred; that by 1910 the operative power myth systems in Britain no longer supported the pretensions of the hereditary aristocracy; that the real power of the House of Lords had already evaporated and that the struggle leading up to the Act was necessary only to make the fact apparent to and acceptable by all. With actual power relations out of line with the myth systems that have supported them, it requires a war or similarly intense conflict to reveal the new situation and establish the new conceptual systems it demands.

This notion is not far removed from Clausewitz's idea of

[2] In "Politics and World Order," an unpublished paper prepared for the Center for the Study of Democratic Institutions.

war as "settlement day." National power is hypothecated on existing military resources, much as commercial transactions are hypothecated on bank reserves. Diplomacy relies on these military "reserves" of power to attain its ends. But when one side or another has overextended its real power, it takes a war to demonstrate the fact, just as it takes a "settlement day" to reveal the true balances of commercial power. "Battle is the payoff," as the common saying goes. It does not decide the issue; it records the decision and makes it acceptable to all involved. The Franco-Prussian War would seem to provide an almost perfect illustration of this concept; and it may be applied, perhaps more dubiously, to the Second World War. After the Locarno settlement in 1925, the operative myth system in European international politics included a France that, with British support, with her alliance systems and military establishments, was "dominant" on the Continent and in particular over the Weimar Republic, whose "power" seemed comparatively exiguous. But by 1939, Hitler was challenging this; he was claiming, in effect, that the Locarno myth system was no longer in accord with facts and that he had developed German military, political, and economic "power" to the point at which "dominance" was in fact in the hands of Germany. How valid was this claim? There was no way of testing it except by war. "Battle" was the only available "payoff," and the payoff duly took place. It finally turned out that the claim was invalid; but this test result was achieved at so enormous a cost in human and material values as to lead us now to question the real significance of the original issue.

So far as it goes, this analysis of the international power problem is no doubt sound—at least for a highly militarized system like that in which we live. One still has the uneasy feeling that it does not go very far. It is profoundly pessimistic, for if an abstract concept of "power" is the final determinant, and war the only means of establishing recognized and acceptable international power positions, there would seem to be no escape from the ultimate and now catastrophic payoff. The fact that a theory is pessimistic does not, of course, mean that it is invalid. But by raising "power" to this abstract level, it gives us no better or more usable definitions than we had before. If it can explain the great wars that have occurred, it cannot explain those that have not, under seemingly similar provocations. It identifies national power completely with national military might, in a context in which it is obvious that there are other factors entering into any nation's power position—as, for example, in the case of India or Canada or the new African states vis-à-vis the former colonial "powers." It does not in itself give us any reason why the goal of abstract power must ultimately be fought for on the international stage by lethal and unlimited military action, when intergroup power struggles are constantly being waged on lesser levels, often with great ferocity but by nonmilitary and even nonviolent means. In this it resembles Karl Marx's prediction of the savage class war. Marx could foresee the group struggle for power, which ultimately took place; he could not foresee the many devices through which it was in most parts of the world resolved without bloodshed.

The theory bases a whole concept of international relations upon a mystical absolute—a Platonic ideal—as impossible to define as are the absolutes of "justice," "truth," or "beauty." We construct our international myth system around the concept of "power," when no one can say with any accuracy what is the power of its major elements—the United States, the Soviet Union, China, or the others—or where the limits of these powers may lie. To say that the fate of men and nations rests upon shifting balances of "power" is to say that it rests upon balances of indeterminables that are also incommensurable. This is not a happy or satisfactory position. To apply power theory at all to the modern world, it would seem that much more refinement is necessary. The power struggle goes on every day among individuals, groups, and states, generally by nonmilitary and usually by nonviolent means. Granted that politics is the organization of power, and that men's affairs ultimately turn upon the way it is organized, why is it that only when one reaches the level of the nation-state is the struggle subsumed into the form of international war, waged to lethal ends with the most extreme and deadly weapons? Why does the behavior of the nation-state in power struggles differ so drastically and bloodily from the behavior of lesser groups?

The usual answer is that on the international level there is no "rule of law." It is true that in all lesser societies virulent power conflicts are worked out by nonviolent means. But this is possible only because they take place within the frame of a sovereign and coercive rule of law, which forbids violence and offers alternative methods for settling the power "disputes" that arise. It seems obvious that to abolish war, the same rule of law must be instituted on the international level, with an international sovereign having the coercive force to forbid resort to violence, empowered to declare the law and supplying judicial machinery to interpret it as "disputes" arise. But it is questionable whether this really meets the problem. There is, of course, a very large corpus of international law in existence today; its rulings are, in most relations of international life, generally accepted; it does not have behind it the coercive power to enforce nonviolent methods of settlement, but it is these nonviolent methods that are normally used. In other words, we already have a reasonably well-functioning system of international law and order. The critical case does not arise out of practical "disputes" between nations. In our highly organized modern world it is rarely if ever that such concrete disputes can be regarded as the "causes" of war; at the most they serve only as triggers to set off the great tests of absolute or abstract "power." It is this abstract character of the international power struggle that has rendered it insusceptible to resolution by a "rule of law" and has made it impossible to establish an international sovereign with the coercive power to enforce peace.

It may be said that only on the international level does "power" assume its ideal or absolute form. John Courtney Murray has argued that the concept of "power" is meaningless unless it is related to some end the power can accomplish. Power to do what? And in most struggles between individuals or groups for the prize of power, there usually seems to be a definite end for which it is designed to use the prize when won. An industrialist may want "power" to "run his own business in his own way"; the Secret Army in Algeria sought "power" to prevent Algerian independence; a revolutionary, like Lenin, may demand power to shape the institutions of his country into new forms that seem good to him. But as one goes up the scale of power organization, the ends appear to become more and more attenuated. Hitler wanted the power to "dominate" Europe, but never made it at all clear for what ends the domination would be employed. The power struggle between the United States and the Soviet Union seems to be an almost pure struggle for power for power's sake. Both nations are today basically conservative (within their different frames of reference); neither is demanding world power in order to revolutionize world relations, even though each passionately suspects this in the other; there are no revolutionaries of the stamp of a Napoleon or Hitler rising within either to utilize the military power of the state in furtherance of their own power ambitions. The "power" that each state strives to conserve is no longer a power to accomplish any specific end; it has evaporated into a mystical absolute—into a power, which is not given in this world, to be safe, secure, untroubled by interference from others and capable of crushing anyone who obstructs one's own desires. This sort of "power" is not only nonexistent; it is also nonnegotiable. A power struggle directed toward finite, or at least concretizable, ends is subject to rational resolution. A struggle for abstract power is not; it cannot be compromised or mediated; it can be resolved only by force and usually only by force in its maximum form—"force without stint or limit," as Woodrow Wilson said in committing the American people to this kind of power struggle in 1917.

It may be argued that this abstraction of power on the international level is a consequence of the success of the nation-state as a means of organizing power. As it slowly established its domestic monopoly of force, it imposed a similar monopoly of all national force exerted upon the world stage. In the more loosely organized past the free-booter, the smuggler, the "merchant adventurer" carried on their own form of foreign relations and foreign war, with no more than the general support of their national governments. Such operations often had a great effect upon international power relations; the East India Company, for example, conquered India as a commercial operation. The nation-state has long since suppressed this kind of enterprise; it has forced its citizens to accept its monopoly of international as well as of domestic force, and savagely suppressed those disinclined to do so. It is now the supreme agent of "power" on the international stage, and any individual or group who for any reason hopes to better his own fortune or power position through international action must do so through the "power" of his state. The "power" of one's own nation thus becomes a generalized, more abstract concept; something like "water power," for example, available for any one of countless uses, but not ordinarily thought of in connection with any particular use. As one's nation's "power" rises on the world scale, the horizons of all individuals and groups within it appear to widen; and if war is necessary to register and retain the national power, war of even the deadliest character must be accepted as inevitable. All this may explain why the modern international power struggle is unresolvable except through war. But it opens a new possibility: that the power struggle itself is losing its significance as world organization has improved and that "power" in the abstract is no longer worth fighting for—certainly not worth fighting for with thermonuclear bombs.

The community of nations—a community composed of only about a hundred individuals, of whom only a dozen stand out—is not like a numerous community of men. Not for a long time, if ever, will it be possible to establish a generalized rule of law going much beyond the law and order we already possess. The struggle for power, on all its innumerable levels, is inherent in human nature. No system of law can eliminate it; no system of law, even on the domestic level, can establish more than a rough approximation of "justice" or do much more than provide nonviolent means of reaching accepted conclusions as to shifts in the ever-changing balances of "power." Accepting all this, one may still say, however, that *military* power, as it has been developed by the elaborated organization of the modern state, no longer has any practical uses except in the search for power for its own sake; that power for its own sake is an impracticable goal; and that the great national power centers may come to lay it aside in favor of the pursuit of other forms of power that may really be of some utility to their peoples.

It is the dethronement of *military* power as between the great states, not the elimination of all power struggle, that is the critical factor in this. Signs are not wanting that the process is taking place. The most obvious is the deadlock over Berlin, in which each side appears to realize that it lacks the military power to force the other to accept its position. Both are now trying to exploit other forms of power— diplomatic, political, propagandist, economic—to bend the outcome to its wishes, but at the moment the most likely result would seem to be an accepted compromise solution. It will have to express the new power balance in Central Europe, but it is likely that both sides will agree to the new balance without putting it to the test of a "settlement day" that must involve a suicidal war.

Another sign, less often noticed, may be found in the power conflict between the Soviet Union and China. There seems general agreement that such a power conflict exists; there seems no less general agreement that it is most unlikely that it will ever be put to the test of war between the two great Communist states. Another sign, of a somewhat different character, may be found in the confusions over the "struggle for outer space." Outer space is commonly represented as the field of a power struggle between the United States and the U.S.S.R. Here is a great technical-scientific venture in which we cannot "afford" to fall behind. There are some who regard this struggle as a part of the terrestrial arms race, who are thinking of it primarily in the unutterably grotesque terms of military satellites and satellite-launched thermonuclear bombs. To most, however, it is not a contest in these crassly murderous instrumentalities of terrestrial destruction. It is the great world of space and science that beckons, not that of war. It is an echo of the tremendous impact of the Russian Sputniks in the fall of 1957. The Sputniks, in themselves, posed no military threat. What they did was to demonstrate unsuspected powers in Russian science and technology, Russian social organization and industrial productivity, all of which could potentially enhance her military "power" but immediately enhanced her "power" in the world in many nonmilitary ways. Nor do many of those who urge us on now to similar achievements in space, who appropriate billions to NASA in order to get our men first to the moon, who seem to think our "power" rests upon success in the enterprise, as yet relate any of this very closely to the bloody, earthbound military process.

The race for the exploitation of space is often compared with the race for the exploitation of the oceans in the sixteenth and seventeenth centuries. It is a singularly poor comparison. The oceans at that time were exploited primarily for economic profit (of which space offers no possibility whatever); secondarily, perhaps, for territorial aggrandizement (again not offered by space) in which profit and military power motives were perhaps combined; and as a poor third for the more purely military motives of gaining bases and windward positions from which to levy war. Aside from the distant (and inhuman) possibility of mounting satellite bases from which to discharge thermonuclears onto the earth, there is almost nothing of all this in the contest for space. The exploitation of the oceans may have represented rather accurately a military power struggle between the Spanish, French, British, and Dutch in the sixteenth and seventeenth centuries. The exploitation of space represents nothing of the kind. It is largely senseless except as a cooperative effort among all the great scientific powers; its real rewards are not those of conquest, tribute, or trade balances; unless it becomes totally debased by the multi-megaton rocketeers, it will represent a nonmilitary contest for what is essentially a nonmilitary form of "power."

The dethronement of military power in the world has begun; if we can avoid disaster along the way it may be expected to continue. In the contemporary world there are no military adventurers comparable to Mussolini or Hitler. The military adventurers of course exist, but they have been confined by the historic process to the smaller powers and to those disorganized areas of the world in which their efforts are unlikely to have much effect on the stability of the total world order. The world has actually developed a power structure to which organized great-power war has become largely irrelevant, and it is not unreasonable to suggest that the organized war system will ultimately fall into desuetude.

While there is no precedent for such a result, on at least two occasions in the Western world something like it has occurred. The power struggle between Communists and non-Communists of today is often compared with the two great periods of "religious" war, between the Christians and the Muslims in the Middle Ages and between the Catholics and the Protestants in early modern Europe. Both were framed around religious faith and conviction, but there can be no doubt that both were power struggles, in which the faiths and convictions served much more as the engines of power rather than as its objects—much as the struggle between Communists and non-Communists is framed around quasi-religious beliefs concerning the nature of man or the quality of justice or the character of the economic system, none of which is likely to be affected in fact by the outcome of the power struggle that rages around them.

The most significant thing about these two earlier power struggles is that each came to an end, and an end that involved neither the total destruction of one side by the other nor the total destruction of the fabric of international order in which they took place. And while they were fought out over the centuries by military means, neither ended in military "victory" nor was either decided by the numerous "decisive" battles that took place in their course.

The struggle between Muslim and Christian was certainly not "decided" at Tours or Granada or Vienna, any more than the modern world problem was "decided" at the Marne in 1914 or at Hiroshima in 1945. Such bloody trials were not unimportant; but in the end the struggle simply declined into a situation in which the growing power of the West— not only military power but economic, technological, intellectual, and organizational power—finally overwhelmed the Muslim world. The power position, which showed a relative equivalence at the time of the Crusades, had shifted into another case of the weak no longer being able significantly to challenge the strong and the strong no longer being fearful of what the weak could do. The Muslims retired into their North African and Middle Eastern bases, and the Christian West swept past them to capture and colonize most of the globe. Wars, of one sort or another, continued between Christian and Muslim states, but the Christian-Muslim War itself was over; it no longer offered a practicable base on which to organize the power relations of the international society.

The power struggle represented by the "religious" wars of the sixteenth and seventeenth centuries also reached its end, declining in this case not into a great disparity but into a rough equality of power. The "decisive" battles that occurred, like that of the Armada in 1588, may have set limits beyond which the respective powers could not reach, but they did not decide the issue between them. The Peace of Westphalia in 1648 was a compromise peace, or stalemate; the Catholic and Protestant powers in Europe were left, as such, in a state of balance, and the religious issue ceased to provide a viable base for the organization of international power in the Atlantic world. There has not been a "religious" war since then. The wars, of course, went on, but they went on upon a greatly reduced level of total commitment and savagery; they were fought over less lethal issues of commerce or colonial territory or dynastic interest, and it was only the development of the war system itself into the hypertrophy of the Napoleonic and the later modern period that produced the seemingly insoluble crisis of power we face today.

But can one say that in theory it is insoluble? Is the goal

of absolute power, in the abstract, any longer the end of statesmanship? Is the "co-existence" of the Communist and non-Communist worlds any more impossible today than was the co-existence of the Catholic and Protestant worlds after 1648? The Peace of Westphalia was based on the principle of *cuius regio*—the religion of the sovereign will be accepted as the religion of the people. This did not put an end to proselytizing by either Catholics or Protestants thereafter, but it removed the question of faith as a serious factor in international politics. Protestants regarded, and long continued to regard, the Catholic faith as non-Communists now regard the Communist faith. Catholicism imposed notions of God and the nature of man and society that to the Protestants were wrong and therefore evil. As an authoritarian religion, moreover, Catholicism *imposed* these notions; it allowed no room for that freedom of inquiry and difference of opinion that were the glory of Protestantism (as it is of liberal democracy today). To a Protestant it seemed that once a community had fallen under the control of Catholicism it was as permanently irretrievable as we now believe to be the case with a state over which Communism takes power. Nevertheless, the principle of *cuius regio* was accepted in 1648 as the basis for a viable international power system; the contesting religions continued their struggle with each other, but the struggle no longer seemed relevant to international politics. Disabilities were removed from Catholics in England, for example, without the English feeling it necessary to demand equal treatment for Protestants in Spain. After the truce of 1648 the ideological issue faded into the backgrounds of the power issue. The longer the modern military stalemate continues, the more likely it will be that the modern ideological issue will similarly recede.

But if it does, what will remain? In the later seventeenth and eighteenth centuries there were quite concrete issues of economic and dynastic advantage, important in themselves to the rival states and quite susceptible to resolution by organized war. There could be "victory," and intervals of "peace" could be built upon it. The war system, as has been earlier suggested, worked. Since 1870 there has been no real victory (if one excludes certain minor and colonial-type operations) and no real peace in the Western world. But there has been less and less to fight about. Gross national military "power" has become increasingly meaningless except in the context of an ideological "struggle," which is as much subject to resolution in the long run as were the religious wars that ended in 1648. While power conflicts of an inordinately complex kind go on every day somewhere in the world, we have in fact achieved an organization of power throughout the globe of a very high order, operating almost wholly by nonmilitary, and in very large measure even by nonviolent, means. As the great weapons systems have been rendering organized war increasingly impossible, they have been rendering it increasingly superfluous. Military power in itself is no longer a goal worth the slaughter of men by the millions or even by the hundreds of thousands to attain. The three or four great centers into which active military power has been successfully gathered have no reason, except their mutual fears of their own weapons, for fighting one another. Neither economic opportunity, markets, raw materials, nor even political power goals are any longer accessible to them through organized war. Each reasonably autonomous, self-sufficent, and invulnerable to the others, the only power contests that have much meaning for them are those that may be carried out in the attempt to influence the uncommitted and relatively underdeveloped areas of the globe, and these are not contests that can be decided by organized great-power war. They are certainly not contests that can be decided at all by the multimegaton war of universal destruction. A demilitarized global power system seems theoretically quite possible. It remains only to ask how, from a more practical viewpoint, it may come about.

CHAPTER NINE

THE END OF THE WAR SYSTEM

FOR AN ANSWER TO THE QUESTION ON WHICH THE PRECEDING chapter closed, one may begin with the situation as it now exists. We have an almost infinitely complicated power structure in the world, largely nonviolent but by no means wholly so. In its innumerable ramifications it turns at times on law, at times on mob violence and guerrilla war, at times on popular votes, at times on military and police dictatorship, at times on propaganda or economic pressure, and often on varying combinations of all these factors. The whole complex structure "heads up," however, into some four major centers of military power: the United States; its Western European associates; the Soviet Union; its Chinese and lesser Communist associates. Only on this final level does one meet the intractable problem of power for power's sake.

On all the lesser levels power-hungry men and groups of men grasp for power, by whatever means, violent or nonviolent, may be open to them, for more or less specific and describable ends. By whatever means they may work, however, they must operate within the framework of the overall international power structure. Today, as in the past, the international military power structure represents a kind of ceiling beneath which all lesser power struggles must be conducted. That is what has always given national military power its absolute and transcendental character. It really has no ends, except to ensure the power of the individuals and groups within the nation. The most formidable members of the primitive tribe could not project their power upon the outer world except to the extent to which the tribe was "powerful." When in 1870 France and Germany contested the "hegemony" of Europe, it was not for any specific purpose in either nation; it was for each an effort to create a situation in which the individuals and classes within each —the politicians, the soldiers, the businessmen, the farmers, the workers—could carry their own internal struggles for power onto a larger stage and enlist the national military power in their support upon it.

Repeatedly through the centuries powerful men within a state have attempted to utilize the state's power to advance their own claims to wealth or authority; and the power of the state (normally expressed in military terms) has at once abetted them and set limits upon their expectations. The more abstractly "powerful" the state, the more opportunities for wealth or specific power seemed to open before its citizens; a decline in state "power" appeared to close avenues previously available. That the appearance might be largely illusory has been pointed out repeatedly since Norman Angell wrote in 1910, and would seem to be amply confirmed by the history of the many militarily weak but rich and prosperous states that one finds in the modern world. Yet the illusion persists. All lesser power is subsumed in national power; the national power becomes an absolute, a transcendental quality, from which all lesser powers derive, and it is the organization of great-nation abstract "power" that determines the organization of all power throughout the globe.

As has been said, a power struggle on this abstract plane is insusceptible to negotiation or resolution. But is there really any need for a struggle? The great-power organization of the modern world has reached a rather remarkable degree of stability. The four great power centers that have developed are largely self-contained and self-sufficient; each has developed a degree of internal order and cohesion that renders it largely impervious to subversive attack from the others; with the development of the great nuclear weapons systems each is largely invulnerable to military assault. In none are there important elements that see in a major war a possibility of enhancing their own power or position within the state. In China and in the Soviet Union, as in Western Europe and the United States, it is apparent that a major war can only destroy the power of the existing governing groups; while the incitation of such a war offers no promising avenue to power (as it did to Hitler) to those who would challenge them from within. The "ceiling" established by the great-power organization is today generally accepted, and the local struggles for power that will continue may be expected to continue within its limitations. The ideological drive for Communist conquest of the world cannot be furthered by major war—certainly not by a major war using nuclear weapons. Great-power rivalry by the "nibbling" process of subversion and guerrilla war is still continuing in such areas as Southeast Asia, and may appear elsewhere. But the outcome, which turns upon many local political and power struggles as well as upon outside interference, is not really being controlled by the now paralyzed military forces of the great power centers; and it is unlikely to unsettle the basically stable power organization at which the world has arrived. In a world demilitarized to police-force levels, struggles of this kind—which might well continue—would be even less likely to do so.

If one accepts the thesis that there is no great war making in the Western world today, and no underlying reason for one except a struggle for power in the abstract, which is meaningless in present contexts, one can look without undue alarm on the continuance of local power rivalries and power struggles in the less organized, less developed, and "uncommitted" world. The underlying problem of power is not insoluble. Africa, Southeast Asia, and Latin America will follow their own destinies; these will be affected by, but will not be controlled from, Moscow or Peking or Washington, and however tangled, difficult, and even bloody these destinies may be they will not decide a great-power struggle that already, to a far greater extent than most seem to realize, has been resolved in the tacit agreement to "co-exist." In the real world of today, organized international war with thermonuclear arsenals becomes not only inconceivably horrible and atrocious, but superfluous. With the very high degree of social organization we have achieved, the great powers (with, of course, the wisdom and assistance of the militarily less powerful states) can quite satisfactorily operate our global community without resort to mutual suicide. We have already developed an adequate power organization as a base. It is only our fears of the giant weaponry and our belief in the mythical goal of power for power's sake that blind us to the fact.

The fears and myths can alike be overcome, and probably will be. One cannot chart today any plan or program—universal disarmament or world government or any other—that can be "adopted" now and that will *produce* this result. One can, it is believed, predict with confidence some of the steps and processes through which it is likely to come about. The first step is a final liquidation of the Second World War. Aside perhaps from Formosa, the question of Berlin and the Germanies is almost the only dangerous crevasse remaining from that immense upheaval. Sooner or later it will have to be closed; and it can only be closed in a recognition of the now existing power balances. In most of the other great issues created by the war—in the Baltic states, Poland, Japan, the Balkans, Greece, Austria, Czechoslovakia, North Korea, North Vietnam—we have accepted the new power structure; whether the resultant agreements were "just" or not can be endlessly argued, but that they were in accordance with the newly established balances of power is hardly deniable. If there is no real great-power conflict across the lines thus demarcated, they are likely to prove stable. Unless we are to undergo a third and final world war, the same kind of settlement must be reached in the Germanies. And in mid-1962 a working settlement seemed to be coming at least within sight. With the liquidation of the Second War the future will be free to make its own history much as it was after 1815.

A second step must surely come with a cessation of the technological arms race. This does not mean general disarmament in the first instance. It does mean a retardation and ultimate cessation of the present insane competition to produce constantly more superdestructive weapons—weapons that, becoming more and more frightfully dangerous in themselves, can have no function other than that now being performed by the weapons we already possess, which is the prevention of war. This competition in arms (as distinct from the arms themselves) is admittedly very difficult for statesmanship to deal with; yet there are signs that it may still prove manageable. The Russians cannot go on indefinitely harping upon total disarmament as the answer to any and all problems without beginning to realize that a stabilization of the weapons systems we have is an obvious prerequisite to their general abolition. General disarmament will never come unless the existing arms systems can be neutralized into a state of inutility.

The Russians, suffering under their own internal political

and power problems, have made less contribution toward this end than it would seem they might have done. But they have made some. The tacit agreement to refrain from the absurdity of competitive civil defense is an instance. This seemed threatened by President Kennedy's resort to military diplomacy in 1961, but good sense reasserted itself and the agreement has apparently survived. The breakdown in the test-ban negotiations in the spring of 1962 seemed a tragic reversal; but again, it may not be the end of the story. The Russians tested in the fall of 1961; therefore, we had to test in the spring and summer of 1962. Yet President Kennedy's avowed willingness to suspend our series if the Soviet Union would accept a controlled ban at least suggests that the purely military gains of the two series were not too important; and there is some hint, through the heavy curtains of censorship, that the military gains in further testing may be subject to a law of diminishing returns.

One is shocked by the scientific calm with which the strategic-scientific-technological students consider such things as hundred-megaton weapons systems, wars in space, satellite orbiting bombs ready to be dropped at command on any point on the earth's surface, and similar extremes of mindless horror. Strategic technology may be panting after such wonderful toys. But as Donald G. Brennan, a very reasonable man, observes in a recent paper [1] on the military effects of outer space: "We should most emphatically not build weapons systems in which a single accident could destroy

[1] In *Outer Space,* Lincoln P. Bloomfield, ed. (Englewood Cliffs, N.J.: Prentice-Hall, Inc., 1962).

perhaps half a continent." If this seems understatement, one has his further remark that so far as he is aware, "neither side presently has orbital bombs under consideration." The technical difficulties are mounting up, leaving the practical strategy farther and farther behind. In discussing the suggestion that multimegaton rockets might be stored on the moon, triggered for release in terrestrial warfare, Brennan points out that the enormous technical difficulties are unlikely to be overcome in any near future; within the same time, "the need for additional invulnerability is unlikely to reach the level at which lunar-based weapons systems seem attractive. The problem is practically certain to be dominated by political considerations." That the lesser weapons problems of today will increasingly be dominated by "political" considerations to which the weapons themselves are irrelevant seems not impossible.

The technological arms race of today is in fact a phenomenon as novel in human experience as is the technology itself. In past arms races the weaponry and manpower has normally been accumulated in the full expectation that it would be *used;* and the technology, while of steadily increasing importance, was not in itself dominant. In the late 1860's, when France and Germany were girding themselves for the struggle (regarded by both as inevitable) that came in 1870, Herr Krupp offered his new rifled steel field guns freely to the French Army. They were rejected (rather mistakenly) on the grounds that French technology was equal to the German. It was the mass of mobilizable manpower that was going to count. Much the same thing was true in the years before 1914, when the British were building "two keels for one" against the Germans, and the French were expanding their army service to keep up with trained German manpower. It was numbers that mattered, not the military technology, which seemed on about an equal level everywhere, and most of which was quite freely accessible to all parties in the coming struggle.

In the modern arms race, numbers have become next to nothing; technology is everything, and the technologists themselves do not really expect to fight the war they so carefully design. How far technology actually rules our lives and how far human needs are still capable of asserting themselves against its fundamentally inhuman dictates are obscure questions. It is probably not true that anything that has once been invented will certainly be used. But at all events, the technologists—the loose amalgamation of scientists, engineers, and soldiers in whom we have been forced to deposit control of our lives and our futures—are themselves passing out into an orbit, so to speak, in which the state of weightlessness is already beginning to trouble them. This is a working amalgamation; they are all in the same capsule, even though allusions to tight association with the military are often irritating to the scientist, who prefers to cling to the myth of the free, unfettered scientific community, dedicated only to the common good and without responsibility for the uses society makes of his insights.

The facts are, however, corroding the myth, even for the scientist himself. Everyone is aware to some extent of the hundreds of laboratories and plants created for and supported by government and manned by tens of thousands of physical and natural scientists working cheek by jowl with lesser folk on specific assignments to achieve specific and immediate technological ends. Almost as visible are the fourth and fifth generations of scientists who have never worked on anything but weaponry and who view their careers as a lifelong dedication to the creation of a succession of exotic weapons systems stretching through foreseeable time. These talented men are institutionalized, captives of a benevolent (and war-oriented) government in the same way that other groups throughout modern history have found themselves "constitutionalized" by kings and parliaments when their expertise, mystique, or special equipment was required to perpetuate the ruling institutions.

They are formidable. They are dedicated to the glory of the great weapon systems rather as the Church is dedicated to the glory of God. But they are not dedicated to war— in which again they resemble the churches, despite all the religious wars the latter have instigated and waged. They are not dedicated to war as was, for example, the elder von Moltke, who spent a life passionately consumed by the hope of military victory. The new arms race is not at all like the older ones, and the new amalgam of soldiers-scientists-technologists is not at all like that which engineered German victory in the 1870's. As has been suggested, the new amalgam already finds itself in a kind of political stratosphere that would have been inconceivable to von Moltke, and is by no means happy in it. Not a few are already in a state of inner revolt that suggests the possibility of turning the great scientific-technological talents that have produced the modern arms race into channels that will give greater possibility of curbing and ending it.

The strategically inclined are already more interested in weapons stability than in weapons mastery, more interested in "deterrence" than in "victory." Many of the purely "scientific" are already interested in the social consequences of their technical achievements—as such journals as *The Bulletin of the Atomic Scientists* or, for that matter, *The Scientific American* demonstrate; as well as in the fascination of their technical researches. The contemporary world presents to both the social and the physical sciences immense challenges —far greater and more significant than the challenge to produce better and therefore more useless weaponry—which science-technology would much prefer to pursue (provided it was paid on the lavish scale the weaponeers enjoy) and which holds out much less barren hopes.

Modern scientific-technological strategy is like a growth, obeying its own laws, following its own ends, and as difficult to control as any growth. But in the modern context it is clearly a cancerous growth, and can be diverted— by the scientists, by government, by a society still capable of seeing some end to the human story other than suicide— into healthier patterns. If one can accept the fact that it is the great systems that are pressing their nominal masters to destruction, it follows that the systems need to be changed. Specifically, one might ask whether it is not possible to build into the framework of democratic (and totalitarian) governing processes advanced technological systems that will give us a better understanding of the world as a whole and of the management of its power relations.

There is no doubt that the sheer problem of communications is one of the most difficult in the modern world; it is also one most susceptible to attack by both the social and the physical sciences. President Kennedy's various gestures in the fall of 1961 toward civil defense, mobilization of reserve forces, and so on, cost $300 million. Obviously useless for waging an actual war, all this was designed to *communicate* to the Kremlin; it was well said that this was one of the most expensive telegrams in history. If mobilized to the task, the physical and social sciences between them can produce less costly, more efficient, and much less dangerous ways of telemetering the fears and aspirations of the world than is provided today by the people who have elevated themselves into "operations analysts" and who try to predict the probable reactions of the "enemy" by an elaborated guesswork that, without much if any real scientific basis, still profoundly affects the gravest decisions of history.

Kenneth Boulding has made the arresting suggestion that our actual knowledge of the processes of international politics is about on a par with our knowledge in 1929 of the processes of economics. The statistical series now at the hand of every economist did not then exist. As late as 1931 people were still arguing whether we were in fact in the grip of a depression; whereas today every change in the economic balances is immediately and sensitively recorded and at the approach of possible depression every alarm bell is set ringing. Nothing like this exists in the international world; we have no way of knowing (and neither do the Russians) whether a tough article in *Pravda* on Berlin is the beginning of total disaster or represents merely a minor "shakeout" of the international exchanges. Nor do we (or the Russians) know this about a tough article in the New York *Times* or the Los Angeles *Times*. The physical scientists are today far ahead with communications and weather satellites designed to transmit information in unheard-of quantities. Science as a whole is far behind in the problem of what information to transmit and how to get it from the tapes and telemeters into the minds of peoples and statesmen. A grant of a few hundreds of millions from government might stimulate science to come up with answers to the latter problems even more useful than those it is coming up with to the former.

This is not to ask for an overlaying organization of scientists to tell us what to do and how to do it but only to point out to the individual scientist (now immersed in weaponry or his next fifty years at Bell Laboratories) that science and its common-law wife, technology, have bathed long enough in the adulation of the popular press and that the awe in which they have been held by great segments of the society for their creation of impressive murder machines is beginning to run out. Now they must, first as men, second as vehicles of a peculiar expertise, turn to inventions of far greater complexity, novelty, and importance. The creation of the thermonuclear war machine has, in a profound sense, stultified international order and crippled our hopes to revive it by traditional military, political, and social means. Science, physical and social, must somehow furnish us with a new system that will function under the actual conditions of the new world science has largely made.

Science in general is reluctant to face problems of the magnitude it has created. For one thing, they are too hard. For all its awesome façade, science now likes to do easy things. A large portion of the community of physical scientists has been immersed for years in the polishing of insights now two decades old or more. The behavioral and social scientists, bemused by their access to electronic calculating gear, each year load the professional magazines with projects of increasing triviality. But this is certainly not the end of the great enterprise that arose with the Renaissance and has produced such stupendous triumphs since.

If the remaining problems from World War II can be resolved; if the great weapons systems can be stabilized to a point at which they will really succeed in their function of preventing any major war over the next dozen years, at least; if the ablest of the world's scientific and technical brains can be diverted from the Gadarene slope of weaponeering down which they are now rushing, into the great problems that really matter—problems of global health, of global food production and distribution, of the global economic order, of improving the content as well as the volume of global communications, of the real nature of power on the international stage, of how military "threat" actually operates upon the minds of those it is supposed to influence—

one cannot doubt the emergence of an even better foundation for a demilitarized international political system.

In two "great debates" before each of the two world wars, the United States argued its course in the highly unrealistic terms of whether to "go in" or "stay out." The question was irrelevant to the history we hoped to control; it was argued with almost no factual data concerning the consequences that might actually flow from either course, and while the argument no doubt helped to shape our subsequent reaction it did not determine the issue, which in both cases was decided by the potential enemy. Our domestic political processes, to which we submitted our course, were simply unsuited to deal with the international politics of the time. Similarly, our course in face of the Great Depression was made the subject of a violent internal political struggle comparatively irrelevant to the real issues involved. Only after the experience, as Boulding remarks, was the factual data accumulated that has enabled the political process to deal much more adequately with such economic problems. We still, of course, have clashes of economic power and interest—politics is, in large measure, the resolution of power problems—but they can be resolved today, we feel reasonably confident, without the enormous suffering and quite needless waste of the early 1930's. The Second War and the weapons revolution has left us much better informed about the basic factors in international politics, and opened great opportunities for the improvement of the information we have acquired. Sooner or later it will become apparent that basic international power problems can be resolved without the suicidal destruction of a major war. As this fact does become apparent, we shall be on the road to an international political system from which major organized war has been eliminated, because we shall be on the road to seeing that major war has become an anachronism—comparable, let us say, to chattel slavery or to the myths concerning unfettered free-enterprise economics.

We are, indeed, on the first stretch of that road already. As William V. Shannon has put it, [2] "World politics in the last dozen years may be roughly defined as an attempt to work out the ground rules for political conflict in the thermonuclear age. Since the nature of nuclear weapons makes it too dangerous to escalate conflicts into major wars, these conflicts have to be considered in a different light than heretofore." One of the two most important emerging issues "posed to politics by technology is how to accommodate and articulate existing conflicts without recourse to war." This reconsideration of the political and power problem is going on in many ways. Here, for example, the West too often overlooks the ultimate implications of the endless Soviet insistence upon general and complete disarmament as the solution for all international problems. This may, as the West suspects, be no more than propaganda. Yet Khrushchev cannot propagandize the outer world without indoctrinating his own people as well; and whatever he may ultimately hope for from his disarmament policy, the fact remains that he is indoctrinating the Russians in a concept of world

[2] In an unpublished paper, "Politics," for the Center for the Study of Democratic Institutions.

history to which major war and mass bloodshed are irrelevant. The Soviet Union can pursue its aims without
these instrumentalities. In the modern power struggle they
are unnecessary to it. No one can predict history with
precision, and Khrushchev cannot know any more certainly
than anyone else where a demilitarized international power
structure would lead. But he proclaims his willingness to
take his chance on that. There is no clear reason why other
statesmen should not more and more incline to the same
view.

Again, the multibillion dollar rush into "outer space"
has its suggestive aspects. It may yield (to adopt current technological slang) a certain amount of "fallout" in the way of
improved rocket motors, guidance and photo-reconnaissance
systems that could have military application but is not in
itself a military operation. This has caused a certain amount
of embarrassment to the ardent and vocal advocates of the
adventure into outer space. They are inclined to play down
military aspects that are in fact too horribly grotesque for
serious public consideration, yet are unwilling to sacrifice the indispensable fuel to be derived from the international power competition; and they are annoyed if
anyone suggests that the whole enterprise is actually only
a scientific-technological undertaking that should, above
all, be binationally or internationally conducted and controlled (as was the International Geophysical Year) if its
true potential benefits are to be realized. But if outer space
must be competitively exploited as an element in the
power struggle, the result is still to transform the struggle

from one in military weapons to one in nonmilitary, prestige values.

The moon has almost providentially appeared to supply an object of expensive international rivalry that is quite useless (except for the contributions it may make to cosmology and geology), and difficult to conceive of, from any practical viewpoint, as a source of terrestrial war. Another was offered by Antarctic exploration, which has now been successfully demilitarized by international agreement. One suspects that other, similar situations will continue to arise—particularly in the relations of the stable great powers to the underdeveloped areas. It is not wholly insignificant, surely, that the Soviet Union and the United States are declared to be in basic agreement on the neutralization of Laos under a coalition government.

All these things are beginnings only, but they are pregnant beginnings. If we can stabilize the organized war system over another couple of decades, and so preserve our civilization from the enormous explosive powers it is storing up, there will be some chance to change fundamental attitudes toward international politics and to dissipate the bloody myths in which we are still bound. It will be seen that major war is not only monstrous but really superfluous to any real needs of the modern great society. We have got on very well without it since 1945, and the vast changes that have taken place since then in the world power and political structure have taken place, in the main, without its assistance. We tend to believe that these changes have occurred without disaster only because of the appalling threats stored in the great military machines; but really scientific analysis of the history and power problems of the period might indicate that the belief has as little foundation as did earlier war myths.

It is today almost impossible for practical, responsible statesmen and politicians, military men, weapons engineers, strategic "analysts," industrialists—to say nothing of publicists, commentators, and "opinion leaders"—to accept the fact that organized war and military threat are alike obsolete. We cannot "trust" the Russians any more than the Russians can "trust" us. We would like to be rid of the ultraperilous weapons systems, but we can make no move in that direction that might "imperil" our own safety. We cannot even make a unilateral declaration that we do not intend to put orbiting bombs in space without an ironclad and "inspected" guarantee from the Russians that they do not intend to do so either, though every calculation from the real factors in international politics indicates that the effort would be a gruesome absurdity from the point of view of either power. The substance constantly escapes us (and perhaps Mr. Khrushchev as well) while we wander in the mythology of our own creation, not daring to look at our world as it actually is, or to conform to the patterns of national and international action that it is almost certain to impose, quite regardless of whether we do or do not "trust" anybody. But these patterns continue to emerge from the misty present. Sooner or later they will be recognized and respected everywhere, just as were the many new patterns of economic and political order that emerged from the Great Depression. Then, and not until then, the great revolution in the international order will move toward its denouement, and the abolition of the organized war system, which today we are forced seriously to think about, will become a practical possibility that we shall find ourselves realizing in fact.

CHAPTER TEN

CONCLUSION

It is now possible to recapitulate. This book began
with the thesis that the world has arrived at a point at which
it is possible to think soberly and realistically about the
ultimate abolition of organized war. It did not promise, nor
has it attempted to provide, a plan or program through
which this result could be brought about. War, like many
other obsolete institutions—human sacrifice, the slave economic system in ancient times or chattel slavery more
recently, feudalism, the unregulated *laissez-faire* exploitation
of wage labor, the divine right of kings, and many more—
will disappear as it is generally understood to have lost its
social value. Such basic institutional changes cannot well
be planned or programmed in advance. Any attempt to do
so must be bogged from the outset (as was Alexander II's
emancipation of his serfs) in the existing power, property,
and political relations that must be altered if the institutional

change is to occur. Any set program for the abolition of war today must suffer under similar disabilities. Necessarily constructed out of the facts of the present, it cannot take account of the quite different facts of the future. Rooted as it must be in what appear to be the "facts of life" as we see them now, it must (to take one example) insist upon rigid "inspection" and "control" of arms agreements in order to design a world order in which neither inspection nor control can really matter. If the new world order can get along without these things, they are unimportant to its design; if the new order must have them, then there is really no new world order and we are back where we began.

Again, most "plans" of this kind, analogizing from existing internal power structures, begin with the assumption that an international juridical system with coercive powers to settle international "disputes" is indispensable to a demilitarized world order. In this the planners are trapped not so much in the present as in a now rather distant past. Modern wars do not arise over international disputes—for the settlement of which a very extensive juridical machinery already exists—but over power problems that are not readily susceptible to juridical settlement and could not be resolved by coercive "enforcement" even if an international juridical system with coercive powers existed. A demilitarized international politics need not and probably will not include a coercive juridical system for the settlement of disputes. The international differences that will continue to arise will be resolved by the same legal and diplomatic mechanisms as are now available; but the underlying global power structure will be such that the irresolvable power problems—most of them military power problems—need no longer enter into international politics.

It is for these reasons that this book has offered no plan or program for producing a demilitarized world order. What it has tried to do is to identify and emphasize these factors in our international society that make it probable that the major international war system will ultimately be laid aside as a salient instrument in international politics. To this end it has tried to make several points:

The first is the collapse of the war system as a foundation for international politics. The collapse was fairly evident in America in 1865; it was confirmed (though only obscurely) by Europe's experiences in 1870-1871; it was demonstrated beyond question in 1914-1918, and made final in the Second World War, with Hiroshima to clinch the argument. By August, 1945, major war had ceased to be practical politics for anybody.

The second point is that the system, impractical as it is as an instrument of international politics or power policy, is growing through the seemingly "autonomous" and mindless force of technological development at an appalling rate. Unless the common attitudes and assumptions that nourish it at the roots can somehow be cut off, it *must* develop into a totally destructive cancer. The big weapons must get bigger; the existing "overkill" capacity must multiply into a still greater hypertrophy of killing power; things like the super-colossal, superexpensive, and superdangerous shelter programs or the possible perversion of "peaceful" space probing into a contest for military control of the universe—all are logical consequences of the whole system and must come unless the system itself can be suppressed. Basically a product of science and technology, these gigantic schemes must sooner or later destroy us, our science and our technology as well, unless the students of politics and the scholars of the social and physical sciences can somehow turn their talents to arresting its grim advance.

The third point is that, considering the degree of social and economic organization to which the modern world has arrived, a demilitarized world politics is entirely practicable. Perhaps the greatest bar to its attainment is the deeply held belief that it is impossible and Utopian. Under the political, social, and economic conditions of the sixteenth century, no doubt a demilitarized international system *was* impossible. But we do not (except in backward imagination) live in the sixteenth century. In the twentieth such a system of international relations has become possible; as time goes on it will grow more possible still. We already have a world power structure that encourages it. The greatest problem today is to convince men of this fact. It is not to design "constitutions" for the warless world—such constitutions, as has been said, will be rooted in present concepts inapplicable to the future—but to inculcate the conviction that a warless world, whatever its specific constitution may be, is a feasible and attainable end.

If all the great military systems were eliminated tomorrow, we would still get along about as we have been doing under the beneficent effects of the nuclear stalemate, but at much lesser risk of total incineration. History would not, of course, justify all our individual hopes for it—but, then, history never has. The United States might not become supreme in the universe; the world might not become totally democratic; some fears as to the character of the future might be realized, but so would a good many hopes. This is the most that the future has ever offered to mankind; and if the demilitarized world presents a prospect in which we must accept bad with good, this is no more than the common human lot, and one that is at least a good deal more acceptable than one that promises to release the equivalent of thirty-five tons of TNT on every soul upon the globe. This is the great point—the core of the whole argument of this book—that a demilitarized world is a practical possibility. If only this point can be persuasively established, most of the rest of the discussion tends to become secondary.

But if secondary, it is not unimportant. The fourth point we have tried to make is that the transition from the present military organization of international politics to a nonmilitary one is not impossible of achievement. Revolutions, even revolutions of the magnitude this implies, do occur. Men's ideas do change; even the most ancient of social institutions undergo modification; concepts (like the concept of hellfire) that seem indispensable in one age to the maintenance of social order and morality are laid aside, to be superseded, in another, by new concepts more suitable to new times and conditions. This process is visibly going on today. If it is not interrupted by the great military catastrophe (and most students now believe that such a catastrophe can be produced only by diplomatic or political "accident"), it is likely to go on to the end. And the end is the demilitarized world.

No one can plot the precise course of this development, but it is possible to advance some rather persuasive guesses as to how it is likely to proceed. "Power" is accumulating, and will continue to accumulate, in the four or five great centers—the United States, Western Europe, the Soviet Union, China—each internally so well organized and so nearly self-sufficient that there are really no power issues between them. These centers, militarily mutually invulnerable and no longer imperiled by subversion instigated from without, are relinquishing, and will continue to relinquish, the idea that any one can or should destroy any other. They are separated today by ideological differences that are not subject to resolution by military force; for the rest, their mutual hostility derives more from their excessive weaponry than from any more concrete clashes of national interest or ambition. They all have available many ways other than those of war for putting their "power" to the test—means ranging from the competition to put a man on the moon to the competition to finance the underdeveloped areas to competitive propaganda or prestige factors. The really basic interests of none can be furthered by military struggle—certainly not by a struggle waged with megaton bombs—and call, on the contrary, overwhelmingly for global cooperation—in scientific technology, in economics, and in political order—if any is to enjoy the potential benefits of which the future gives promise to all.

To predict that from this evident situation there will arise a nonmilitary global organization of international politics does not seem unduly reckless. This was, in fact, the prediction upon which the far from softheaded or Utopist diplomatists of 1945 founded the United Nations. A generation before, the League of Nations had been established on an essentially military concept of international relations—all the powers would, to some extent at least, retain their military armaments and peace would be assured by "collective security," which is to say the collective use of military weapons. The principle relied upon in 1945 was different. Its core, enshrined in the "veto" provisions of the Security Council, was great-power unanimity. There could be no doubt as to the kind of international system this implied. At the time and repeatedly thereafter it was explained that the United Nations could not deal with a war or threat of war among the great powers. It could operate effectively, in short, only in a warless world—warless, at least, so far as the great powers were concerned. Power would be concentrated (as in fact it has been) in four or five great centers; such a power structure would leave them with no reason for fighting or fearing one another; military action would become irrelevant in their relations, and the Security Council, working under great-power "veto," would be adequate to preserve order in the world.

In the succeeding seventeen years such expectations were not, of course, to be realized. Yet nearly everything that has happened since 1945 has been forcing us more and more clearly toward this as the only possible solution for the world problem. How else can a working international power system be organized except through this concentration of power in a relatively few great centers, each unafraid of and militarily unthreatening to the others? The only obvious alternative is a global concentration under a single "world government" with coercive legal authority over all states, groups, races, and associations—something impossible today and, even if it became possible, probably far less workable, desirable, or just than the situation envisaged by the authors of the United Nations. The 1945 solution is still the only one anyone has been able practically to suggest. Every day serious statements multiply to the effect that this is the situation to which the world must come; and none finds any answer to them beyond a perpetual balance upon the knife-edge of mutual nuclear suicide.

President Kennedy has committed the United States to the goal (advanced by the Russians) of general and complete disarmament. But what else could he commit us to? Khrushchev had advanced at least three fundamental propositions in regard to modern international politics, on all of which the West has looked with the deepest suspicion, but for none of which the West has found any real answer. To none have Western sources proposed any alternative that makes lasting sense. The first, of course, is general and complete disarmament. The frightened howls the West has raised over this specter cannot affect the fact that it is ultimately the only practicable outcome. Our only modern alternatives are total disarmament or total disaster. The West is well justified in saying that it cannot accept a disarmament that will leave it helpless before an uncontrolled Soviet military power. It is not justified in a refusal to admit that a total disarmament represents the only rational future for the international system. It laments the supposed propaganda successes Khrushchev has achieved with his "GCD," but it cannot make similar propaganda successes on its own for the simple reason that it has developed no design for a viable future of which the great weapons systems remain a permanent feature.

Khrushchev's second proposition is that nuclear wars must be ruled out as suicidal; that "limited" wars on any large scale must be excluded because they are certain to escalate into thermonuclear wars, and that there remain only "wars of national liberation"—civil and guerrilla conflicts in the less ordered parts of the world—which the Soviet Union reserves the right to influence in the interests of its ideology and of Communist "freedom." The West has responded very angrily to this as simply a device to ensure Communist conquest of the globe through infiltration and "indirect aggression." But the West has no answer to the very real problem here posed. It cannot seriously argue that all "wars of national liberation" must be rigorously suppressed henceforth, with all peoples of the globe confined to the straitjackets they happened to be wearing in mid-1962. The West knows very well that there will probably continue to be minor violence, wars, riots, and disturbances of one kind or another. Having committed itself to the great weapons systems whose only function is to prevent any war whatever (but which are quite helpless to affect events in places like the Congo or Laos), what better answer can it offer for this problem? The Western assumption that "wars of national liberation" will always end in Communist victory does not do much credit to Western energy and confidence; but if the West has any more hopeful way of meeting this issue it has failed to produce it. Our own current strategic arguments about "brush-fire" wars, the "missions" of our Army and other ready forces, the proper place of the reserves in our total military posture, all reveal the inability of current political and military policy to deal with the problem of "wars of national liberation," which is to say with the problem of unavoidable change in a demilitarized world.

A third of Khrushchev's basic propositions is that if major war is excluded, the world order must be organized on a "troika" system or something like it. He has suggested that as the world approaches the crux of the power problem, a tripartite organization—to include the organized West, the organized Communist system, and a neutralist third force—offers the only presently possible way of dealing with it. Again, this has caused angry outcries in the West with charges of Communist bad faith and duplicity. But the outcries have been unaccompanied by any more practical answer to the underlying problem. If it is not to be met in somewhat this way, how is it to be met? The heavily unbalanced voting in the United Nations General Assembly disqualifies it as a legislature; while even if the votes were equalized in accordance with population or power, in some such way as has been suggested by Clark and Sohn, the ultimate result would seem to be not far from Khrushchev's "troika." Otherwise, one must accept a power organization based either on Western destruction of Soviet and Communist power or Communist destruction of Western power. Such possibilities have become the merest fantasies in which no responsible statesman, not even Khrushchev, any longer seriously indulges.

The broad concept of a world generally demilitarized to police-force level, from which major war has been excluded, in which riot and guerrilla wars may be expected to continue in the less settled parts of the globe, but the effects of which can be reasonably controlled by a substantial coalition of the great-power centers, is a more practical and credible one than any other that has been presented. To more and more thoughtful minds, everywhere in the world, it is coming to represent not only the most desirable but the most probable outcome. Generally speaking, we have already excluded great-power war as an instrument of national policy. We are coming close to excluding the *threat* of major war as such an instrument. Threats of this kind may still be necessary— though obviously very dangerous—instruments of communication; but the policies that may be communicated in this way are not policies of war. As has been suggested, President Kennedy felt it necessary in the Berlin crisis to mobilize two National Guard divisions, encourage an absurd shelter program, and take other martial steps, in order, as he said, to provide a "capability" large enough—not to wage war, for all these measures put together were ridiculous as preparations for an all-out war over the Germanies—but "to *make clear our determination* and ability to defend our rights at all costs." [1] This is not war but communication; it is the politics of the dawning international order, not its military

[1] Address of July 25, 1962.

strategy. It displayed a "toughness" which may (or may not) have had psychological effect in the Kremlin—Russian strategists could hardly have overrated the military importance of the measures taken—but even this kind of thing will more and more be laid aside as its dangerous irrelevance to the real problems of power come more and more to be recognized. In the subsequent Cuban missile crisis "toughness" again seemed to produce results, but it was toughness which fell far short of threatening war. Both sides were still in the realm of communication, not of armed combat.

With the great nuclear strategic stalemate we have heard more and more about peripheral threats, "brush-fire" wars, and secondary "emergencies" anywhere in the globe to which we must be ready to rush conventional forces at the drop of a hat. But situations of this kind are not really controllable, except within certain quite narrow limits, by great-power military action. In the Indochina collapse the United States refrained from landing troops or deploying atomic bombers, neither of which would have been appropriate to the resolution of the actual political problems involved. In Cuba we stopped with supporting an emigré invasion; and the resultant fiasco was no encouragement to the landing of American troops. In the two latest and most dramatic of our military exploits, the landings in Lebanon in 1960 and in Siam in 1962, we were very careful to land only on the invitation of the local government and only where there was no actual fighting. This is probably a quite rational employment of military power in the new world that is taking shape around us. To enter with force of arms a country already shattered by subversion, rebellion, and guerrilla war, in which, as in Laos, there is no cohesive local government or strong popular support, is to play a loser's game. To buttress a more stable situation before the infiltration and guerrilla warfare has begun is a considerably more profitable but considerably less warlike utilization of military force. It is a discharge not of a military but of essentially a police function (not too unlike that of the United Nations troops in the Congo) that can be adjusted to the actual power structure in the modern world—as Soviet support for our Laos policy, including the preventive landing in Siam, seems to suggest.

War, even of the peripheral variety, is becoming less practicable, and its threats less politically useful or credible in the international order as it already exists. The terrible mass-destruction weapons are stalemated, and conventional armed forces, where they are used at all, are used more and more in much the way that the national and proposed international police forces of a demilitarized world would be employed. These facts are unlikely to escape the statesmen or even the publics of the great nations as time goes by. The great defensive military systems will initially be maintained, but at a decreasing pressure of threat that should make it possible to end the competition in new weapons and weapons development and facilitate the stabilization of the deterrent system so as to ensure that it will in fact continue to deter. One can hardly expect that these processes will advance through the usual form of "disarmament" negotiations, which have the uniformly self-defeating consequence of maximizing the very factors they seek to control or eliminate. They will advance, rather, through a mutual search for military and defense policies that can be put into effect unilaterally or by tacit agreement, or by written agreements that are self-enforcing.

A still possible nuclear test ban is only a first example. As the great nuclear powers focus their attention more upon the weapons systems and less upon political and power objectives the weapons, demonstrably, are unable to sustain, other possibilities will open. There has been much discussion, for example, of a formal, unilateral declaration by the United States that it will never again be the first to use nuclear weapons in warfare. Properly presented, this would almost certainly invoke a similar declaration from the Russians, and relieve the world of much present fear and tension. But, it is said, such a move is quite impossible; it would tie America's hands while no one could "trust" the Russians to remain similarly bound. The only result would be to license a Soviet "first-strike" upon the United States, or to license an overwhelming assault by Soviet conventional forces that we would be debarred from meeting with tactical atomic weapons. This is, of course, the ancient stumbling block that has appeared before all efforts to reduce or control armaments. Nor does there seem to be any good answer to it as long as one pins one's whole picture of the future on the supposed power of the weaponry. As the severe limitations upon the weapons themselves in any political or power context become more apparent, however; as it becomes clearer that the weapons are themselves the great problem, rather than political or power issues they can no longer affect, both an American declaration that they would not be used *and* a Soviet concurrence would become considerably more credible. This is not because either side would any more "trust" the other, but because each would see more clearly the parallel interests driving the other to the same end.

There are numerous other ideas for the tacit or self-enforcing demilitarization of the world system, none of which seems very practicable today but all of which may be realized tomorrow. There is the Rapacki plan for the demilitarization and de-atomization of Central Europe. There are suggestions that the Polaris-submarine deterrent system could be restrained within limits that, while no less adequate for defense, would have considerably less offensive potentials. There were the Eisenhower "open skies" proposal to avert "surprise attack." They no longer figure largely in the international discourse, not because they were illogical, but because no one today thinks surprise attack a very serious problem. With the steadily increasing sophistication in the foreign offices, and even in the general staffs, of the great powers, we are approaching a point at which a general demilitarization becomes increasingly possible and at which, as a matter of fact, most of the huge weaponry of mass destruction is simply supernumerary.

If this much is true, and is likely to become more evident with the passage of the years, what will then happen? There are several possibilities. One is that there will be a slipup, the diplomatic "accident" that will destroy civilization. Another is that the nations will divest themselves of their thermonuclear weaponry and go back to a simpler and less destructive war system on something like the old eighteenth century lines. This appears to be the view of Thomas C. Schelling, who argues that even total disarmament could not prevent war, but would simply create conditions under which the nations would rearm and rethreaten each other as they used to do, with similarly lamentable results. But a third view is that the nations and power groupings will simply lay aside the war system altogether in favor of a more workable system of power relations. If this happens, the critical factor will not be through the prior development of a "world law," though law and legal invention will presumably have a large role to play, but through the development of power structures in which large-scale, organized war is no longer seen as necessary or, indeed, relevant.

In the view of this book, the last is overwhelmingly the most probable outcome—quite regardless of the question of whether the prospect seems desirable or not. The human race as a whole is notably resistant to mass suicide; nations may have sustained enormous losses in wars, but they have never in modern times come even close to accepting the total destruction with which the new weaponry confronts them. Humanity has been almost equally resistant to returns toward past sociopolitical systems that have outlived their usefulness; and even those cultural systems that appear to undergo arrest or decline, decline into stagnation rather than into regression. Neither the catastrophe promised by the existing war system nor a revival of past war systems seems as probable as the ultimate elimination of major war.

The arrest of the present insane competition in new forms

of weaponry and a better stabilization of the existing balance
of terror must alike proceed from, and at the same time
reinforce, the realization that the basic power positions of the
great states are increasingly unaffected by their huge weapons
establishments. The longer the nuclear stalemate can be
maintained, the more confidence will grow within the great-
power centers that their security and survival are sufficiently
ensured by nonmilitary power factors. The competitive
pressures behind military technological development will
tend to relax; it will become increasingly difficult to justify
any fantastic new military experimentation on the ground
that it might conceivably yield some military "advantage,"
and increasingly unnecessary to fear any possibility of the
"other side's" making technological gains of which we are
unaware, or which we cannot inspect and control. Today
it is enough to label any technological possibility, however
wild, with the word "military" to enclose it at once in the
protective shrouds of "military security," to ensure millions
and billions for its support, and to put it beyond any rational
criticism; it is enough to detect any possibility of "military"
application in a Russian development to demand that we
instantly match or surpass it, or at least establish inspection
and control over it. Even today, the true military significance
of most such developments is wholly disproportionate to the
fears engendered by and the money spent on them. As the
real inutility of the weapons systems becomes more apparent,
a more rational accounting will be applied to them. What
do the promised (or at any rate the hoped-for) military
advantages really amount to? What are likely to be the

military costs, to say nothing of the political and economic, they are certain to exact?

Accounting of this kind will become more possible, and more effective in damping the arms race and stabilizing the resultant weapons positions. At the same time the social and political sciences will be, as they are being, stimulated to the study of a nonmilitary system of international politics. This involves better communications, a better understanding of the actual forces that operate within any great-power center, of the nature of international "conflict," its limits and potentialities, of the relation between the international power conflicts and the subordinate hierarchy of power conflicts that go on all down through nations, groups, corporations, and individuals. Today, it is taken as unquestioned pragmatic wisdom when someone declares that the "tougher" the attitude on the part of the West, the more accommodating is the attitude of the Kremlin. The observation is certainly not without empirical support; but it is a generalization from so complex a system of actual variables as to be almost devoid of predictive or practical utility. Such crude conceptions in international politics will be broken down, much as the physicists' former conception of the atom as the final and indivisible particle in nature has been broken down into the far more complicated conceptions that have opened the way to the great triumphs of modern physics.

The more the social and physical sciences can turn themselves from the soft yet barren fields of weaponeering technology and the painstaking refinement and reworking of the ancient myths toward the really difficult task of developing the new concepts that make possible a nonmilitary international power structure, the simpler the problems of general disarmament will become. As a nonmilitary system of power relations continues to develop in fact, the task of developing the concepts appropriate to it will become easier. A simple example is provided by the provision in the United Nations Charter establishing a Military Committee to consider an international police force. The provision was wholly nugatory, because in 1945 the ruling myth systems made an international police force impossible. But we have since seen the rudiments of such a force developing as the facts have forced a modification of the myth system. The American intervention in Korea as a "police action" under the flag and auspices of the U.N. may seem an unhappy example; but it did on the one hand further the concept of international police action while it taught us, on the other, much more than we knew in 1945 about the limitations as well as the uses of the concept. The later armed U.N. interventions in Palestine and the Congo were on a very different basis; they were undertaken because events compelled them—there seemed no other way of meeting the real as distinct from the imaginary problems of order—but with a far more realistic appreciation of what could and could not be accomplished in this way.

They were, and are, rudimentary experiments. We still know far too little about their uses in the modern world, about the political order necessary to sustain them, about many of their larger implications, but one can hardly doubt they provide a beginning from which an international police force in a demilitarized world must practically grow. The same is true of the uses to which the great powers have actually been putting their conventional military forces.

If the great forces remain stalemated, if armed power is increasingly deployed upon the world stage only in ways that would be expected of a world generally reduced to police-force level, can the great weapons systems, and the organized international war system of which they are the hypertrophied outgrowth, permanently survive? It seems unlikely. It is true that their (probably gradual) disappearance will create problems. Other uses will have to be found, in all societies, whether Communist or democratic, for the brains, the energies, the natural resources, and the money that is now squandered upon them in such astronomical amounts. But this is a problem that is on the one hand soluble and on the other not of presently critical importance. It is of the greatest value to have the work of the United Nations committee of experts or of Emile Benoit and others on the economics of disarmament. Just as this book has sought to create the conviction that the warless world is politically possible, they have given powerful support to the conviction that it is economically possible as well. There is nothing in either capitalist, mixed, or Communist economics to compel us to accept the ultimate suicide of our civilization.

This it is most necessary to know, but it is a question that has not yet really arisen. It is no doubt true that the economic interest of arms manufacturers, scientific and technological weaponeers, politicians representing arms-manufacturing centers, lead them to cling to and perpetuate the myth systems that accord with their interest. This is an invariable of socio-economic history. It is probably not true that they are any more significant than any other members of the great society in maintaining myths to which all subscribe. It is the myth systems themselves that really count, not those who may to a greater or lesser degree benefit from them. In every revolution, some of the most effective revolutionaries come from the ranks that most benefited from the old regime. Systems are rarely, if ever, upset except by the collusion, if not the incitation, of those who stand at the top of the system. It is a circumstance that lends hope to the plea to the scientific and technical community to rebel against the war system that has profited them most and prostituted and degraded them all.

But one cannot sit back and simply wait for "Science" to close the Pandora's box it has disastrously opened. The governing myths are created by us all, shared by us all, and lay upon all of us an equal obligation to test them, to question them, and improve them. Across the whole problem of war and defense in the nuclear age there echoes a plaintive cry: "This is a dreadful situation. What can I *do* about it?" The only real answer is a hard one: "You can think about it." This book has no program to offer; it does not attempt to start a "movement." Peace movements, rallies, picketings, mass protests have their value in forcing attention to what is the primary problem of our age; but they are unlikely to be of much effect unless and until they can bring people to grapple with the underlying myths—which most participants in peace movements themselves share—supporting the war system. Peace movements have existed in this country for over a century and a half. They were advocating general disarmament on the eve of the Mexican War. Their success has been minimal because they have never freed themselves from the old assumptions or come close to questioning the basic concepts involved in the problem of war and peace.

The time has come when these concepts can be revised, and must be revised. What is needed to do this—in face of entrenched institutions and automatic reflexes whose beginnings are lost in antiquity—is not a "movement" of some kind, but hard thought leading positively toward the construction of the new world order. What is needed is intellectual labor on the part of those who have developed and supported the means by which man may obliterate himself. This kind of thought is demanding. It must ask difficult questions: What is "military necessity?" What is the necessity? What purposes will any given military measure really serve? What political, social, or moral ends will it destroy? How does the international power system operate in fact? What is military power and what are its limitations? This is the kind of thought we must have. We need it from scientists and technologists; we need it from politicians and editorial writers; but we need it above all from the great reservoir of democratic power, the businessmen and workers and average citizens who, embarked in a society that is passing from a military to demilitarized world system, can encompass the new concepts the new system demands.

This book began with the statement that it is today possible, for the first time, to think about a world without war.

These are the lines along which the thinking must proceed. If it does, the warless world will be realized. If it does not, we shall probably all be cremated in thermonuclear war. Of the two alternatives, it would seem, strictly in a predictive sense, that the first is the more probable.

27